Magic Tricks for Grown-Ups

Magic Tricks for Grown-Ups

Jon Tremaine

THOMAS DUNNE BOOKS
ST. MARTIN'S PRESS ✖ NEW YORK

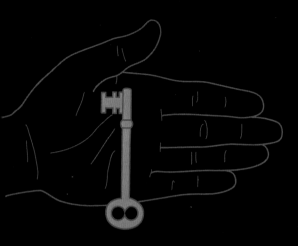

THOMAS DUNNE BOOKS

An imprint of St. Martin's Press.

175 Fifth Avenue

NEW YORK, NY 10010–7848

WWW.STMARTINS.COM

First U.S. Edition: February 2006

Creative Director PETER BRIDGEWATER

Publisher SOPHIE COLLINS

Editorial Director JASON HOOK

Art Director KARL SHANAHAN

Senior Project Editor HAZEL SONGHURST

Design THE LANAWAYS

Illustrator IVAN HISSEY

This book was conceived,

designed, and produced by

THE IVY PRESS LIMITED

The Old Candlemakers

Lewes, East Sussex BN7 2NZ, UK

ISBN: 0-312-34940-8

EAN: 978-0-312-34940-0

10 9 8 7 6 5 4 3 2 1

Printed and bound in China

contents

introd

This book is overflowing with the most amazing magic tricks. They're great to do wherever you happen to be—in the office, in your favorite bar or restaurant, at dinner parties, and at any social gathering where a little light entertainment will really add some sparkle to the proceedings.

Okay, so you won't actually learn how to saw a woman in half or make an elephant vanish—but you will learn some exquisite close-up magic tricks. You can perform most of them impromptu, because the whole concept of the book is to show you how to do marvelous magic with ordinary, everyday objects that you can easily lay your hands on—pens, paper, matches, glasses, napkins, playing cards, and so on.

Once the word gets around that you can do magic tricks, you'll find that people will be drawn to your new showmanship. You might well find that your social life has suddenly improved! You could even impress your business clients and increase your sales. Wherever you are, you'll be able to break the ice and become the life and soul of the party.

uction

Take things slowly: set yourself the task of learning one trick every day. Rehearse in front of a mirror—that way, *you* can see what the audience will see. Only perform a trick before an audience when you feel confident that you could perform it blindfold.

Remember that a magician is an actor playing the part of a magician, so this is your opportunity to sharpen up your acting skills. It's fun to ham it up a little—but don't overdo it, because you want your audience to focus on your magic, not your stand-up comedy.

Technically, all the tricks are easy to do—the difficult part is the PRESENTATION. This is where nearly all the success of the trick lies, so practice is essential. The three most important guides to becoming a successful magician are practice, practice, and yet more practice.

Although magic may not turn out to be your next career move, it is very likely to become an absorbing and fascinating hobby. I sincerely hope so.

Good luck!
JON TREMAINE

magic in
the office

LIFE IS MUCH HAPPIER when you have a good relationship with your fellow workers. Whether you work on a factory floor, on a construction site, or in an office, the ability to lighten the load of the daily routine is always welcome.

That is where magic comes in. Learn a few of these astonishing but remarkably simple tricks and you'll suddenly have an easy and sociable way to break up the working day.

Not only that—if your job is selling, you'll find that the ability to perform a magic trick will do wonders for your sales figures. Your clients might pay more attention to you and you'll be able to get your message across more effectively. You have introduced a magic ingredient in communication—entertainment!

"That was just one of the miracles that our company can perform for you. Now let me introduce you to another miracle product..."

People imagine that you have to be very clever to be a magician, so be cool and never tell anyone how easy it really is—simply accept their admiration and plaudits with good grace.

And one very important thing—never intentionally reveal the secret methods that you use. The motto of the Magic Circle is *Indocilis Privata Loqui*—which loosely translated means, "Keep your mouth shut." Magicians are trained to keep their secrets—but no one else is!

Your colleagues will try to persuade you to reveal the secrets of your tricks. They'll say: *"I promise that I won't tell anyone. How did you do that?"* When anybody asks me how I did it, I usually answer: *"Very well!"*

So make sure that you perform these tricks "very well." Practice until your magic is as good as your company's product!

the vanishing pen

A lesson in the contrariness of inanimate objects.

WHAT THE TRICK IS

You say that you will make your pen pass right through the palm of your hand. Instead—the pen vanishes!

WHAT YOU NEED

A ballpoint pen or a pencil.

WHAT YOU DO

★ You perform this trick standing, with a colleague positioned to your left.

★ Hold out your left palm. Hold the pen in your right hand in the writing grip [FIG.1].

★ Place the point of the pen on the center of your left palm [FIG.2] and state that, on the count of three, you will make the pen penetrate right through your palm and come out the other side.

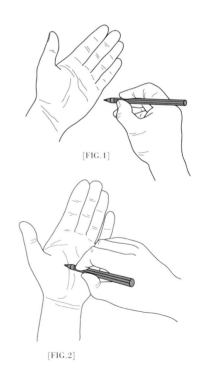

[FIG.1]

[FIG.2]

[FIG.3]

★ Lift your right hand up in an arc until the pen is about at cheek level—then lower the pen onto your left palm again—counting "One."

★ Do it again—this time counting "Two."

★ On the third count, just raise your right hand a little farther and lodge the pen behind your right ear [FIG.3].

★ Bring your now-empty right hand down again to touch your palm as you count "THREE" [FIG.4].

★ The pen has vanished!

★ Say: *"Oh! Sorry! This is the trick where the pen vanishes!"*

★ You can now exit the office crabwise—leaving your hapless victim completely mystified—or you can have a good laugh by seeing how long it takes before they notice the pen tucked behind your ear!

[FIG.4]

the missing link

You can use any dull meeting as downtime to perfect this timeless classic.

WHAT THE TRICK IS

A spectator holds an elastic band and you make two paper clips magically link onto it.

WHAT YOU NEED

A currency note (or a strip of paper if you're broke).

A rubber band.

2 trombone-type wire paper clips.

WHAT YOU DO

★ This crafty trick is self-working, but you must pay great attention to the setup. The drawing will make it all clear.

★ Fold the note in half lengthwise.

★ Thread the rubber band on.

★ Now fix the paper clips in position. It is important that the clips and rubber band are inserted on and through the note exactly as shown [FIG.1].

★ Have the spectator hold the top of the rubber band.

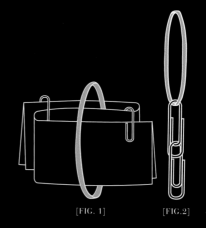

[FIG. 1]   [FIG.2]

★ All you have to do is pull the ends of the note in opposite directions and—hey presto—they are left with a chain of paper clips linked to the rubber band [FIG.2].

★ The fact that the linking happens in the spectator's hands makes this trick all the more effective.

the hypnotized coin

This trick shows that your power can be stronger than anything—even hard cash.

WHAT THE TRICK IS
You borrow a coin and balance it on its edge on your fingertips. Very slowly and mysteriously it lowers itself until it's flat on your palm. You immediately hand the coin out for inspection.

WHAT YOU NEED
A pin or thumbtack.
A large coin.

WHAT YOU DO
★ Secretly hide the pin behind the coin [FIG.1], then conceal the pin in your right hand.

★ Slide the head of the pin between your index and second fingers and grip it very tightly. You should now be able to balance the coin easily [FIG.2].

★ Now—very, very gradually, ease your grip on the pin. The coin will slowly lower itself onto your fingers in a most mysterious manner [FIG.3].

[FIG.1]

[FIG.2]

[FIG.3]

the business card

Do people shrink from accepting your business card? Never again with this trick!

WHAT THE TRICK IS

On the back of your business card you sketch a matchstick monkey climbing a rope rising from a basket. The spectator writes their initials on the basket. The card is then turned over and they initial that side too. When the card is turned over again, the monkey has vanished! In its place is the sign: OUT TO LUNCH! The spectator's initials are still on both sides of the card.

WHAT YOU NEED

A dozen or so of your business cards.
A pencil.
A small but wide rubber band.

WHAT YOU DO

★ On one of the cards draw the OUT TO LUNCH sign, rope, and basket [FIG.1].
★ Place it on the stack of cards and put the rubber band around the middle.

[FIG.1]

[FIG.2]

★ Cut another card in half and draw on the rope and matchstick monkey [FIG.2]

★ Place the half card over the OUT TO LUNCH sign and tuck it under the rubber band [FIG.3]. It now looks as if the top card is a monkey climbing up a rope that is rising from the basket.

★ You are now ready for the trick.

★ *"Have you ever seen the famous Indian Rope Trick? No? Let me show you."*

★ Show the stack of cards with the monkey climbing up the rope.

★ Give the pencil to the spectator and have them place their initials in the basket. Keep hold of the top of the stack while they do this.

★ Turn the stack face down. The card that they have signed is now at the bottom of the pile.

★ Pull this card from the stack and have them write their initials on the back.

★ Put the rest of the cards away in your pocket. The dirty deed is now done. You only have to concentrate on the magical presentation!

★ Pick up their initialed card and—with your fingers covering the OUT TO LUNCH sign [FIG.4]—show them that their initials are still on both sides.

★ Place the card (drawing side down) on the table again.

★ *"In the story of the famous Indian Rope Trick, a rope mysteriously rises up from a basket. A monkey suddenly runs out and climbs up the rope.*

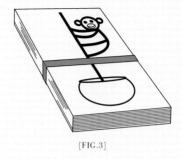

[FIG.3]

[FIG.4]

When the monkey reaches the top of the rope he disappears! Do you know where he went?"

★ *"No."*

★ *"Turn over my card and you'll find out!"*

★ When they examine the card, their initials are still in place, but the figure has vanished. In his place is the sign: OUT TO LUNCH!

★ Apart from being a great little trick, the spectator ends up with your all-important business card. They will want to keep it to show to friends and colleagues. It pays to advertise!

the marriage bands

This one is great when you have a few minutes to spare at the coffee machine. You can use it as a moral lesson too, if you dare.

WHAT THE TRICK IS

You show two separate rubber bands—roll them up into a ball—then the two become one.

WHAT YOU NEED

A thin rubber band.

WHAT YOU DO

★ You are going to hold the single rubber band in a certain way to enable you to display it as two rubber bands. Look at FIG.1 very carefully. This is your starting point.

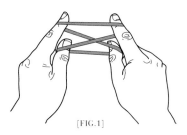

[FIG.1]

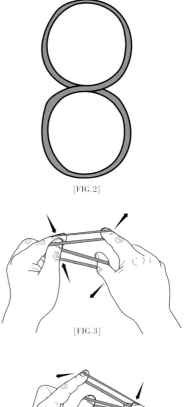

[FIG.2]

★ To achieve your starting point, you must first TWIST the band into a figure eight shape [FIG.2].

★ The index finger and thumb of each hand are threaded into the figure eight EXACTLY as shown [FIG.1]: fingers in the top loop, thumbs in the bottom loop. Now stretch the loops as far as possible.

★ The illusion of the two rubber bands is achieved by pinching one finger and thumb together at exactly the same time as you open the opposite finger and thumb [FIG.3].

★ Now reverse the procedure—pinching the other finger and thumb together at the same time as you separate the other finger and thumb [FIG.4].

★ Do this five or six times quite rapidly and the illusion that you are holding two bands is perfect.

★ End the trick by quickly bringing both hands together, releasing your fingers and thumbs. Stretch the rubber band out to show that the TWO HAVE NOW BECOME ONE. Just like a marriage!

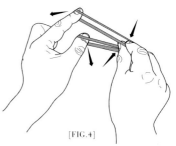

[FIG.3]

[FIG.4]

the impossible penetration

To some people, having a magician push a knife into their money will feel like a knife through the heart!

WHAT THE TRICK IS

You pass a sharp paper knife through the center of a currency note. Afterward you restore the note and show that no harm has come to it!

WHAT YOU NEED

A knife with a sharp blade.
A currency note.
A piece of paper that is a little larger than the note.
A paper knife or a pencil.

TIP

Select a knife with a long, slim blade that slides comfortably inside the narrow slit in the currency note. And remember that practice makes perfect!

WHAT YOU DO

★ To prepare, use a sharp knife to cut a slit in the note. This should be about ¾ inch/2 cm long and ¾ inch/2 cm in from the short edge [FIG.1]. Your audience will never notice this secret slit. Put the note in your wallet or billfold along with your other money.

★ To perform, casually remove the note from your wallet. Show that the note is intact. Keep your thumb over the secret slit!

★ Fold it ALMOST in half. This covers the slit and leaves about ⅜ inch/1 cm overlapping [FIG.2].

★ Now wrap the piece of paper around the note [FIG.3]. Both ends of the currency note should still be visible.

★ Insert the paper knife between the two ends of the note. The arrow in the illustration shows you where. Let the tip of the knife pass through the slit so that the knife actually passes BENEATH the main body of the note and not through it!

★ With a sudden push, pass the knife down and through the piece of paper. If you are careful, you can wiggle the knife about so that a considerable rip is shown in the paper [FIG.4]. The illusion is perfect.

★ After a while, remove the knife and display the currency note fully restored to health!

[FIG.1]

[FIG.2]

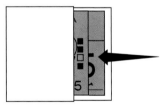

[FIG.3]

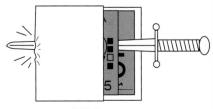

[FIG.4]

the spiked coin

Choose a fairly suggestible subject for this one—it's certainly not for the spiky cynic in your office.

WHAT THE TRICK IS

You press a small coin against the center of your forehead. It stays there. It drops off when you frown. You give the coin to a spectator so that they can try it—but to their horror they find that the coin has a large thumbtack stuck to it! You apologize for the gag and give them another coin. They manage to stick it to their forehead, but cannot dislodge it—no matter how hard they try.

WHAT YOU NEED

Glue or adhesive putty.
A thumbtack.
2 similar small coins.

TIPS

This trick is pure psychology and works on the fact that the skin still feels the presence of an object after it has been removed.

WHAT YOU DO

★ Glue the thumbtack to one of the coins [FIG.1] or use adhesive putty.

★ Conceal this spiked coin carefully in your left hand.

★ Produce the other coin from your right pocket—display it openly between your right finger and thumb.

★ Press the coin onto the center of your forehead and release your grip [FIG.2]. The coin will stay there—held in place by your natural skin oils.

★ Frowning will cause the coin to drop into your cupped right hand [FIG.3].

★ Repeat the stunt, but this time catch the coin in your cupped left hand— where it joins the concealed, spiked coin. Casually reach over with your right hand, remove the spiked coin, place it on the table in front of the spectator, and ask them if they would like to try.

★ Watch their face as they notice the lethal spike!

★ After the laugh, you apologize and show the real coin.

★ *"Let me press it onto your forehead"*

★ Press the coin firmly against their forehead. Twist it slightly, then secretly remove the coin and conceal it.

★ It will be ages before they realize that there isn't a coin there at all and their frowning antics will be most amusing for everyone else!

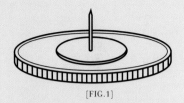

[FIG.1]

[FIG.2]

[FIG.3]

the office pen pusher

A good game to play on the office "pen thief": the one who always makes your pen vanish.

WHAT THE TRICK IS

You ask someone in the office to show you their pen. You examine it for a while, then put it in your pocket. You begin to walk away, saying, "Thank you very much." When they protest, you apologize—then reach up and suddenly produce their pen from behind their ear!

WHAT YOU NEED

A jacket with inside pockets.

TIP

For an alternative ending, thrust your right hand (and the pen) into your right pant pocket. Pull out the pen and say, "Hey! I've got one just like yours!"

WHAT YOU DO

★ This trick is deceptively simple to do, but don't underestimate its impact on the pen owner. Pretend to examine the pen thoroughly when they hand it to you.

★ *"This is a beautiful pen."*

★ Using your left hand, appear to put the pen into your right inside jacket pocket [FIG.1]. In reality, you drop it down the right sleeve. If you cup your right hand, you will be able to catch the pen as it passes down your sleeve [FIG.2]. Begin to walk away…

★ *"Thank you very much!"*

★ They will immediately stop you in your tracks and demand to have their pen back.

★ *"Oh! I'm so sorry! That's a really bad habit I've got into."*

★ Reach up and "produce" the pen from their left ear!

[FIG.1]

[FIG.2]

the french drop

You will already have realized that you needn't be a sleight-of-hand expert to perform interesting and mystifying tricks—but if you take the trouble to master the following technique, it will enhance your tricks and add a professional touch.

WHAT THE TRICK IS

A coin or any small object disappears when transferred from one hand to the other.

WHAT YOU NEED

A coin.

TIP

Mastering the French Drop and "finger grips" to hold coins without appearing to do so are key skills that will help you perform many magic tricks.

WHAT YOU DO

★ Hold the coin in your left hand exactly as shown [FIG.1].

★ Your right hand travels forward to meet it. The right thumb goes beneath the coin and your right fingers go over the coin [FIG.2].

★ You are apparently grabbing the coin, but as soon as it's hidden from view by your right fingers, let the coin drop secretly into your left palm.

★ Complete the grabbing motion with your right hand and close it into a fist as if it contains the coin. Move this hand away [FIG.3].

★ DO NOT MOVE YOUR LEFT HAND! Just grip the coin lightly in a "finger grip" with your second and third fingers.

★ Now, slowly and dramatically, open your right fingers. The coin has simply vanished!

★ Well, that's it. It's very simple to do, but does require a great deal of practice to make it look natural. Practice in front of a mirror. A good idea is to adopt the starting position [FIG.1] and actually take the coin away in your right hand. Study what this looks like. When you perform the French Drop, it must look exactly the same.

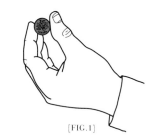

[FIG.1]

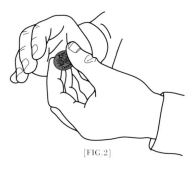

[FIG.2]

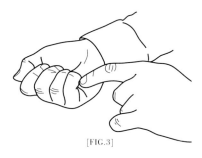

[FIG.3]

the eye of a needle

It may not be a camel, but it's still a surprise when the coin drops through!

WHAT THE TRICK IS

You pass a large coin through an obviously smaller hole in a sheet of paper.

WHAT YOU NEED

A sheet of paper.
A coin.

WHAT YOU DO

★ Fold the paper into quarters.
★ Tear off a piece from the center corner to make a round hole [FIG.1].

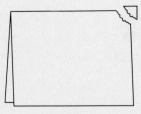

[FIG.1]

[FIG.2]

★ This hole must be noticeably *smaller* in diameter than the coin [FIG.2].

★ Now hold the paper between your hands and drop the coin into the folds. Part of the coin will project through the hole.

★ Grip the sides of the paper firmly and then slowly push your hands together [FIG.3]. This movement has the effect of making the diameter of the hole larger and the coin will pass through the hole.

★ Once the coin has dropped through the hole, open the paper up completely to show that the hole is intact—no tears appear around the hole—and that the camel has definitely passed through the eye of a needle!

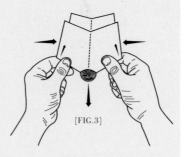

[FIG.3]

the phantom key

Practice hard and one day you might be able to unlock doors from a distance!

WHAT THE TRICK IS

A large, heavy key is laid across your palm. Merely by "concentration," you make it come alive and turn itself right over—just as if some unseen ghost were turning it in a lock.

WHAT YOU NEED

A large mortise key—the heavier the better [FIG.1].

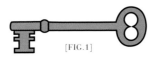

[FIG.1]

> **TIP**
>
> *The success of this trick really depends on your powers of concentration. So don't be afraid to take your time and let the tension build.*

WHAT YOU DO

★ It may take you a few minutes to get the hang of this. Once you acquire the knack, you will always be able to do it—just like riding a bicycle!

★ Lay the key across your palm. The exact position is very important—study FIG.2 carefully. Notice that the flat part that is normally inserted into the lock is pointing back toward your wrist.

★ The other end of the key that has the ring on it must be free from obstruction—not resting on your hand at all.

★ Look down at your hand.

★ Very, very slightly dip your fingers toward the floor and *will* the key to turn over! That might sound silly, but it really does help!

★ Slowly and mysteriously the key will turn over (FIGS.3 & 4).

★ At first the key will turn over very quickly. However, by varying the degree that you tip your fingers, you will soon learn how to control the movement of the key completely so that the turning becomes very slow and mysterious.

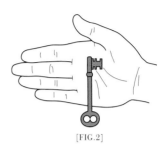

[FIG.2]

[FIG.3]

[FIG.4]

the flying paper clip

Practice makes perfect—and this one takes a lot of practice. Experiment on the bus, in lines, and at any other downtime.

WHAT THE TRICK IS

You show two paper clips, holding one in each closed fist. Instantly, one of the clips vanishes and flies across to join the clip held in your other hand.

WHAT YOU NEED

2 trombone-style wire paper clips [FIG.1]. They need not be of the same size or color.

> **TIP**
>
> *This trick is just as effective using two coins— or any small objects that can be held easily between your lips and "French dropped" (see p.24).*

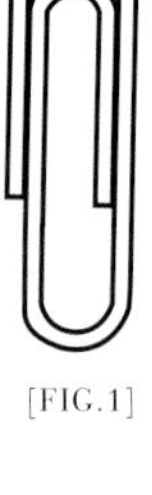

[FIG.1]

WHAT YOU DO

★ Show the two paper clips and display them between the thumb and first fingers of each hand [FIG.2].

★ Raise your right hand and take the paper clip away, gently gripped between your lips [FIG.3].

★ Display the left-hand clip and hold it in position to execute a French Drop (*see page 24*).

★ Now perform the French Drop— apparently taking the clip away in your right hand, but actually retaining it in your left hand. Close the right hand into a fist as if it contains the paper clip.

★ With your left hand, take away the paper clip from your lips and close the left hand into a fist. You now have BOTH clips in this hand, although your audience will be convinced that you are holding one clip in each hand.

★ Shake the right fist as if it still contains the paper clip.

★ Count, "One... Two... THREE."

★ On the count of "Three," smartly open your right hand to show that its clip has vanished.

★ Open your left hand to reveal the amazing transposition!

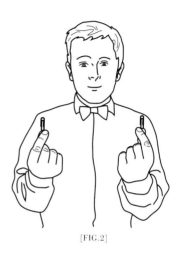

[FIG.2]

[FIG.3]

the spinning note

Your spectators will find their heads spinning when you send a currency note into a whirl.

WHAT THE TRICK IS

You balance a currency note on an upturned pinhead. Then, without touching it, the note begins, slowly and mysteriously, to spin around in circles like a windmill!

WHAT YOU NEED

A long pin or a toothpick.
A lump of adhesive putty.
A currency note.

TIP

Your hands interrupt the natural airflow and cause the note to spin. With practice you can make the spinning note stop, or suddenly spin in the opposite direction.

WHAT YOU DO

★ Set the pin or toothpick upright by sticking it into the lump of adhesive putty (FIG.1).

[FIG.1]

★ Find the center of the currency note by folding it in half both ways.

★ Carefully place the note so that its center is on the pinhead and the note balances [FIG.2].

★ Ask your audience to watch and to concentrate on the note. They must try to make it move just by the power of their concentration.

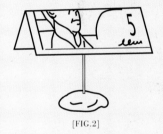

[FIG.2]

★ Hold your hands on either side, taking care that you do not actually touch the note [FIG.3].

★ *"I'm concentrating very hard and at the same time sending radiation from my hands. Look, but don't faint!"*

★ The note should now be moving, and slowly start to spin!

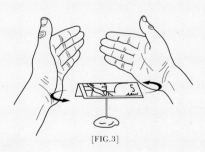

[FIG.3]

the twister

For perfect magic, it pays to have some hidden help. With a secret prop, you'll be able to perform this trick to a tee.

WHAT THE TRICK IS

A borrowed currency note is laid across the palms of your hands. Without warning, it suddenly does a complete 360° turn. You immediately hand it back to its owner, and no cause for this phenomenon can be found.

WHAT YOU NEED

A white golf tee.
Adhesive putty.
A borrowed currency note.

WHAT YOU DO

★ To prepare, shorten the spike end of the golf tee so that it measures about ⅛ inch/1.5 cm long.
★ Fill the bowl of the tee completely with adhesive putty [FIG.1].

[FIG.1]

TIP

This is a startling demonstration of apparent telekinesis. Just don't overdo it. Remember: never underestimate the intelligence of your audience.

- ★ Conceal the tee in your right hand, gripping it between your index and second fingers. The tee is hidden under your thumb [FIG.2].

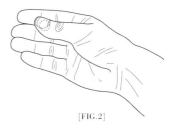

[FIG.2]

- ★ Take the borrowed currency note with your left hand, then place it in your right hand so that it covers the tee. Your right thumb is transferred to the top of the note in the process.

- ★ Press the tee onto the center of the note. The putty will stick the tee to the note so that you can take your hand away for a moment and just hold the note in your left hand [FIG.3].

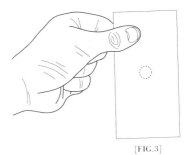

[FIG.3]

- ★ Show that your right hand is empty and place the note along its edge. Bring your left hand, also palm upward, to join the right hand, to make the position shown in FIG.4. Grip the tee between your two hands.

- ★ Retaining a slight grip on the tee, move one hand slightly forward.

- ★ The currency note starts to revolve. Very little movement is needed to make the note spin.

- ★ Discreetly peel off the tee as you hand the note back to the stunned spectator.

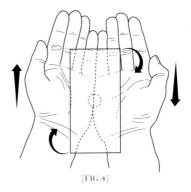

[FIG.4]

the endless thread

*This is my favorite practical joke.
The old ones just run and run!*

WHAT THE TRICK IS

A well-meaning colleague notices a piece of white cotton on your jacket lapel. As they try to tidy you by removing it, they find that the more they pull, the longer it gets!

WHAT YOU NEED

A flat cotton bobbin from a sewing machine, wound with white thread.
A needle.
A jacket with an outside breast pocket.

[FIG.1]

WHAT YOU DO

★ Thread the needle and pass it through your left lapel from inside to outside [FIG.1]. Remove the needle and leave a thread 1–1½ inches/2.5–4 cm long on the outside of your lapel. Pop the bobbin in your outside breast pocket [FIG.2].

★ Before long, someone in the office will try to smarten you up by removing the thread! Great fun: do try it.

[FIG.2]

the bone crusher

A cup could cause a stir for someone who doesn't know their own strength.

WHAT THE TRICK IS

A work colleague greets you with a handshake. A terrible bone-crushing sound accompanies your tortured facial expression and blue expletives, as it appears that they have broken the bones in your hand.

WHAT YOU NEED

A plastic cup from a vending-machine (or an empty sandwich container).

WHAT YOU DO

★ Hide the cup in your armpit, beneath your shirt, and you are all set.
★ Crush the cup as soon as the unsuspecting person grips your hand.
★ You should be able to bring a great deal of pressure to bear on the cup by pushing your upper arm into your body. A horrible cracking, fracturing sound will be heard.

kerr**unch**!

★ This is your cue to act it up for all you are worth! Hop about, blowing on your fingers, as if in terrible pain. Threaten to sue the person. Really ham it up. Thier face will be a picture!
★ It's all very simple, but you will need to practice a little to get the timing exactly right.

magic in
the bar

BARS ARE NOT only a great place for meeting up with friends and colleagues—they are a perfect venue to try out the latest in your repertoire of tricks. Surrounded by people who are there to unwind after a long day or relax on the weekend, you'll have a captive audience that is ready and willing to enjoy the diversion of a little impromptu magic!

Bar magic is also a perfect ice-breaker when you're traveling abroad—you may not speak the language of the country you're visiting, but that's fine, because magic is universal and you'll soon find yourself communicating!

This chapter deals with tricks that are best suited to the bar environment. They all use items that are found in most bars: coins, glasses, bottle caps, matches—even cigarette ash! Whenever possible, use items that you've borrowed from your audience: this really increases the effectiveness of the tricks. Your spectators will have a vested interest if they have provided a coin or currency note, or there's a free drink at stake—they won't know that they'll inevitably end up buying you a drink!

On the downside, your performing angles in these locations are sometimes a little difficult—you will often have people crowding around you, especially as your reputation as a magician grows. Before you "go public" with your bar tricks, practice being smooth and subtle with your moves so that you don't give anything away if someone happens to be looking over your shoulder or breathing down your neck. Choose your tricks carefully.

On the upside, you will find it quite easy to distract people's attention away from your hands whenever you want to. The hustle and bustle of bar life makes this simple.

One golden rule (learned from personal experience) applies when you perform in bars: don't try doing tricks when you've had too much alcohol. I can assure you that there is nothing worse than watching a drunken performer!

the spinning heads

This fabulous bar trick is guaranteed to win you a few drinks... or your money back!

WHAT THE TRICK IS

You turn your back while a friend spins a coin on the bar top. You bet them a drink that you will be able to tell which way up the coin will land six times in a row. Mysteriously, you are right every time.

WHAT YOU NEED

Any round coin (the larger the better). A craft knife.

WHAT YOU DO

⊛ Secretly cut a small nick on the rim of the "heads" side of the coin with the craft knife [FIG.1]. Put the "fixed" coin in your pocket with a few others.

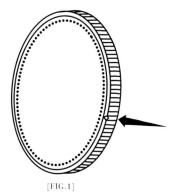

[FIG.1]

TIP

In the case of very suspicious friends, "fix" all the coins in your pocket, then invite them to choose which one to use.

⊕ Place your bets first, then take out all your coins from your pocket. Remove the marked coin and put the rest back in your pocket. This way it seems that you're willing to use any coin.

⊕ Give the coin to your friend and ask them to spin it on the bar top.

⊕ Turn your back while they spin the coin. All you have to do is LISTEN to the rhythmic sound that the coin makes as it finally comes to rest flat on the bar [FIG.2].

⊕ If the coin lands head side up (the side with the nick), then the noise will have a dull tone and will come to a more GRADUAL stop.

⊕ However, if it comes to rest tail side up, there will be a sharp clattering sound, which will stop abruptly.

⊕ All it takes is the ability to tell the difference between the two sounds and you'll never again buy another drink!

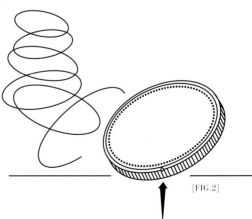

[FIG.2]

the pulsating matches

Here's a quickie that you can perform anywhere. It's very amusing when the audience attempts to copy you—and fails dismally.

WHAT THE TRICK IS

You get a spectator to hold your right wrist and say that you will pick up the beat of their pulse with the assistance of two matchsticks. One match is laid across the other and, without any visible means, one match starts to jig up and down, apparently to the beat of the spectator's heart!

WHAT YOU NEED

Two wooden matchsticks or toothpicks (borrow these if you can).

TIP

Your fingernails are covered in tiny grooves—like an old gramophone record. These grooves are the secret of this simple but effective trick.

WHAT YOU DO

- Hold a match firmly between your thumb and index finger of your right hand. Press it down onto the nail of your second finger [FIG.1].

- Put the second match on your left hand—overlapping your palm and resting on the other match [FIG.2].

- Press down hard on the first match so that it skids on the tiny grooves in your nail. This will make the second match jump [FIG.3]. Keep the pressure up and it will jump at least ten times before you need to adjust your grip to reapply the pressure.

- With a little practice you'll be able to make the second match jump up and down to a rhythm similar to your pulse.

- You could also try laying the second match on a bar top or another person's palm. Bring the first match beneath it and it will jump as before.

- It's almost impossible to see the first match moving across the grooves.

[FIG.1]

[FIG.2]

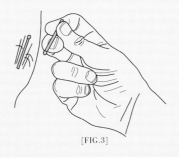

[FIG.3]

the matchbox
acrobat

With a little careful preparation,
you'll find it easy to create a perfect
little prop: a matchbox made in heaven!

WHAT THE TRICK IS

A matchbox performs acrobatics on
the back of your hand—it stands up
and the drawer eerily opens on
its own.

WHAT YOU NEED

About 16 inches/40 cm of transparent
fishing line or invisible thread. (I use
3-lb/1.3-kg breaking-strain line.)
A needle.
A drawer-type matchbox.
A small safety pin.

WHAT YOU DO

✪ Remove the drawer, thread the needle
and pass it through the wall of the
matchbox sleeve from the INSIDE to
the outside at point A. [FIG.1].

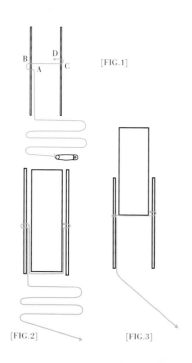

[FIG.1]

[FIG.2]

[FIG.3]

◎ Still following FIG 1, thread back through the wall at point B. Go across the box and out the other side (point C). Thread through the wall again farther up (point D).

◎ Tie a knot in the end of the thread and tie the safety pin to the other end. Insert the drawer from the top and close the box. If you now pull on the thread, the drawer of the box should open halfway [FIGS. 2 & 3].

◎ Attach the safety pin to the inside of your left jacket pocket.

◎ When you're ready to perform, take the matchbox out of your pocket. Place it on the back of your left fingers, with the fishing line passing between your index and second fingers [FIG.4] and from there to the pin in your pocket.

◎ [FIG.5]. Notice how the thread passes between your fingers up to the top side of the box. This is very important.

◎ If you now move your left hand forward slightly, the matchbox should stand up on end (FIG. 6). Push a little farther forward and the drawer will mysteriously open (FIG. 7).

◎ To a fairly observant person, the forward movement of the hand is very noticeable. Get round this by keeping the hand perfectly still and moving your body instead. Just bow over the box or move your left side back a little and you'll get the desired effect.

◎ You may have to shorten the thread a little because you'll find that you don't need too much slack when you're in the correct position.

[FIG.4]

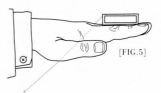

[FIG.5]

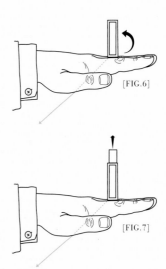

[FIG.6]

[FIG.7]

the psychic coins

This is a staggering demonstration of mind-reading. Did you know I was going to say that?

WHAT THE TRICK IS

You take a handful of coins from your pocket and lay them out in a long line across the bar. While you turn your back, a spectator is invited to point to one of the coins. You turn around and instantly tell them which one they have pointed to.

WHAT YOU NEED

A handful of coins.
A good friend who is "in" on the method and can keep a secret!

TIP

If the spectator tries to fool you by not pointing to a coin, you know that too, because your friend does not sip their drink at all!

WHAT YOU DO

- ⊙ You need a small crowd, so gather four or five people around you at the bar.

- ⊙ They should all be (and most probably are) holding drinks. Your secret partner should be positioned to one side and should only be visible to you out of the corner of your eye. This is quite important.

- ⊙ Lay your coins in a row across the bar.

- ⊙ Invite a spectator to join you in a little mental experiment. Invite them to point to one of the coins while your back is turned. There is no way that you can see what they are doing.

- ⊙ Turn around again and ask them to concentrate as hard as they can on the coin that they pointed to.

- ⊙ Gaze earnestly at the coins on the bar. You should just be able to see your friend out of the corner of your eye.

- ⊙ Now hold your index finger over each of the coins in turn. Try to make this a slow sweep along the line, rather than pointing individually to each one.

- ⊙ When your finger is hovering over the correct coin, your friend takes a sip from their drink.

- ⊙ Yes! It's as simple as that! It's surprising how far you can be facing away from your confederate and yet still be aware of their signal.

- ⊙ Don't reveal the coin at once—make it look difficult. Look as if you really have to concentrate!

TIP

Most tricks should not be repeated to the same group on the same day, but this is an exception. It gains strength from repetition—about four times should do it!

the rip-roaring rip-off

Money tricks are always popular and this trick with a borrowed currency note is a real eye-catcher! It's brazen magic at its best.

WHAT THE TRICK IS

You borrow a note and, to the spectator's horror, very openly and definitely tear it into four pieces. Apologize and screw the pieces up into a ball. When you open up the balled pieces again, they are joined together. The note is fully restored and no worse for wear. Phew!

WHAT YOU NEED

A pen.
A currency note of the same value as the one that you intend to borrow.
Clear sticky tape.

WHAT YOU DO

- Put the pen in your right jacket pocket.
- Screw your currency note into a ball and conceal it in your left hand.
- Ask a spectator if you can borrow a currency note of the same value as your concealed one.
- Take the note in your right hand, then transfer it to your left hand so that it conceals your palmed note [FIG.1].
- Hold the note up in front of you.
- *"It's amazing how strong money is. You can be really rough with it and it won't rip."*
- Tear the note down the middle and display the two halves—one in each hand [FIG.2]. Act as if you are as upset about the situation as the spectator.

- *"Oh, no! I'm so sorry!"*
- Put the right half on top of the left half and rip them up again.
- *"This isn't supposed to happen!"*
- Screw the four pieces up into a ball and press the ball onto the concealed screwed-up ball in your left palm. You can hold the lot between your left finger and thumb and it will look as if it is one torn and balled-up note [FIG.3].
- Take the bundle away between your right thumb and index finger [FIG.4]. This reverses the notes so that the whole one will now be on top.
- Take the top part back with your left thumb and index finger—leaving the torn bundle between your right finger and thumb.
- Your right hand should immediately go to your right jacket pocket. Dump the torn pieces. Bring out the pen.
- *"I'll have to use my magic pen."*
- Using the pen like a magic wand, tap the balled-up note three times, then return the pen to your pocket.
- Blow on the note, then slowly unravel it to show it fully restored.
- Practice these moves with plain paper until you can do them smoothly.
- The spectator will recoil in horror when they see you ripping up their note. Later, in private, retrieve the pieces and stick them together again using the sticky tape. Line up the pieces with great care and stick them from the BACK. Your note will still be legal tender in this form.

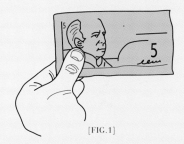

[FIG.1]

[FIG.2]

[FIG.3]

[FIG.4]

the chink-a-chink

With a few beer-bottle caps, you can give a demonstration of incredible sleight-of-hand. It's easier than you think.

WHAT THE TRICK IS

Four bottle caps are displayed on the bar top. Your hand covers one. Another one vanishes and appears under this same hand. The other two caps disappear in turn and also reappear under your hand.

WHAT YOU NEED

5 beer-bottle caps—the type with scalloped edges. The audience is only ever aware of four of them.

TIP

If you are in a restaurant, you could try this routine with sugar cubes. You can palm them almost as easily as bottle caps.

WHAT YOU DO

○ Practice palming a bottle cap. Put one on the table, scalloped side up [FIG.1].

[FIG.1]

○ Place your right hand over it so that the bottle cap is positioned in the direct center of your palm.

○ Press down and squeeze the sides of your hands inward a little [FIG.2].

[FIG.2]

○ Lift your hand off the table and you should be able to take the bottle cap with it [FIG.3]. The sharp scalloped edges make this easy to accomplish— it's surprising how little movement of your hand muscles is needed.

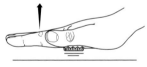

[FIG.3]

○ Now try it with your left hand. When you're happy that you can palm a cap well with either hand, you can progress to the following routine. It will be a star trick in your repertoire.

○ Start with the secret extra cap palmed in your right hand.

○ *"This trick is called Chink-a-Chink."*

○ Lay the four visible caps out in a square formation [FIG.4]. I have labeled the positions A, B, C, and D to make things clearer for you.

"Chink-a-Chink looks like this…"

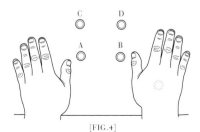

[FIG.4]

○ *The Chink-a-Chink trick is continued on the next page.*

the chink-a-chink

☼ Cover "A" with your left hand and "B" with your right hand. Wiggle the fingers of both hands a little. Drop the palmed cap so that it joins "B," and at the same time palm "A." Move both hands away to show that "A" has apparently magically jumped across to join "B" [FIG.5].

"Sometimes it looks like this…"

☼ Move one of the caps at "B" back to position "A." Cover positions "A" and "B" again. Wiggle your fingers. Drop the cap that you still have palmed in your left hand to join the cap at position "A" and at the same time palm the cap at position "B" in your right hand. Move both hands away. The cap has apparently jumped back again (FIG.4, *see page 51*)!

"Although it usually looks like this…"

☼ Form the square formation again and repeat the transfer of "A" to "B" [FIG.5].

☼ *"Occasionally it looks like this…"*

☼ Cover "B" with your LEFT hand and "C" with your right hand [FIG.6].

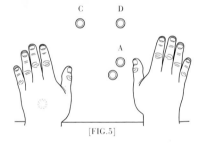

[FIG.5]

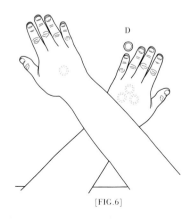

[FIG.6]

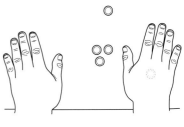

[FIG.7]

- Drop with your left and palm with your right. Move your hands away. Three caps now show at position "B" [FIG.7].

- *"Although once in a blue moon it looks like this..."*

- Cover "D" with your left hand and the three caps at "B" with your right hand [FIG.8].

- Palm at "D" and drop at "B."

- Move your hands aside to show all four bottle caps at position "B" [FIG.9].

- Well, that's it! Please practice until you can perform the series of moves smoothly and at a moderate pace.

- Don't worry too much about the remaining bottle cap still palmed in your right hand. Just slip it into your pocket at an appropriate moment.

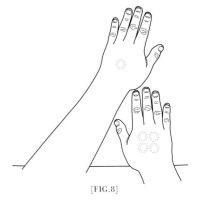

[FIG.8]

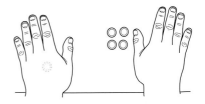

[FIG.9]

the dashing ash

Even cigarette ash can be put to good use with this spooky spectacle.

WHAT THE TRICK IS

You cause cigarette ash to appear in the palm of a spectator's closed fist without, apparently, touching them.

WHAT YOU NEED

An ashtray with ash in it.

WHAT YOU DO

- ✪ Moisten your right thumb and grind it into the ash in the ashtray: you will find that a small quantity will stick firmly. Do this long before you start the trick.
- ✪ Ask for a volunteer.
- ✪ *"Hold your hands out in front of you, with the palms up."*
- ✪ Grasp both their hands [FIG.1] and turn them face downward, pressing your thumbs firmly into their palms. This action transfers a quantity of ash onto their left palm without them knowing.
- ✪ *"Close your hands into fists."*

TIP

The secret of this trick is in the presentation. The sleight of hand is over early on, then you just have to concentrate on selling the magic!

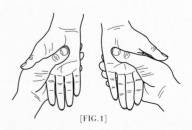

[FIG.1]

- They form their hands into fists [FIG.2]
- *"Keep your hands closed until I tell you otherwise. I'll try something you will think is stupid. Please humor me. Could someone find me an ashtray!"*
- Take a pinch of ash between your right thumb and index finger and sprinkle it on the back of their RIGHT fist [FIG.3].
- *"I'm placing some ash on the back of your hand. I will make the ash travel from the back of your hand to **inside** your hand. Remember—don't open your hand unless I ask you to."*
- Blow the ash off their hand.
- *"The ash is now inside your hand! Don't open it yet. Now—if I can put ash inside your hand, it follows that I can also take it out again! Watch!"*
- Mime a sprinkling action over the top of the ashtray.
- *"Now turn this fist over—open it!"*
- They do [FIG.4]. The hand is empty.
- *"Isn't that amazing? The ash has gone. Close your hand and I'll do it again."*
- Sprinkle ash on their hand again and then blow it away.
- *"This time I'll make the ash dash from this hand, up your arm, across your shoulders, down your other arm, and into your other fist. Don't open your hands yet!"*
- Point at the route the ash is taking, but don't touch your volunteer. The audience will think you've gone crazy!
- Get them to open their right fist. No ash! Ask them to open their left hand.
- Their palm is marked with ash [FIG.5]!

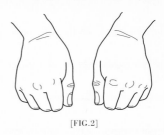

[FIG.2]

[FIG.3]

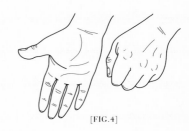

[FIG.4]

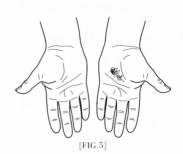

[FIG.5]

the magic pen

Here is another trick that uses the French Drop. It's an impromptu trick for all occasions.

WHAT THE TRICK IS

You borrow a coin and hold it in your right fist. You tap the hand with your "magic pen." The fist is opened—the coin has vanished. The empty hand is closed into a fist again. Another tap with the magic pen brings the coin back again.

WHAT YOU NEED

A pen.
A jacket with inside pockets.
A borrowed coin.

TIP

You can see how the French Drop really enhances this simple but beautiful cameo. Practice the moves until they become second nature to you.

WHAT YOU DO

✪ Start with the pen in your inside right jacket pocket.

✪ Borrow a coin and perform the French Drop (*see page 24*), but keep your right fist closed. The coin is now actually palmed in a left-finger grip.

✪ Dive your left hand well inside your jacket, drop the coin into your right sleeve, and remove the pen as your hand comes into view again [FIG.1]. It should appear as if you have reached inside your pocket to get your pen.

✪ *"This is my magic pen!"*

✪ Tap the back of your right fist with the pen [FIG.2].

✪ *"If I tap the back of my hand once, the coin will disappear."*

✪ Open your fist dramatically to show that the coin has vanished [FIG.3].

✪ Display the pen with your left hand and at the same time drop your right hand to your side—cupping your fingers. The coin will drop down your sleeve and you should be able to catch it secretly quite easily [FIG.4].

✪ Close your hand into a fist again and bring it up to waist level. Tap the fist twice with the pen [FIG.5].

✪ *"If I tap twice—the coin will return."*

✪ Open your fingers and show that the coin has magically returned [FIG.6]!

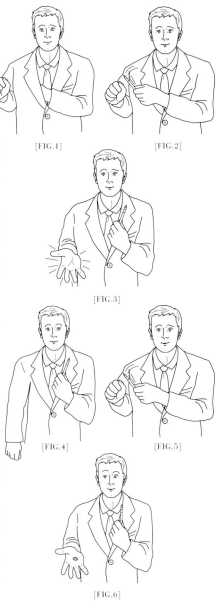

[FIG.1]

[FIG.2]

[FIG.3]

[FIG.4]

[FIG.5]

[FIG.6]

the ring and
shoelace I

Magic on a shoestring—all the fun of David Copperfield and none of the expense.

WHAT THE TRICK IS

You tie a shoelace into a loop. A solid ring suddenly appears as if from thin air in the middle of the loop—threaded on the shoelace.

WHAT YOU NEED

A finger ring.
A long shoelace or string, about 33 inches/84 cm long.

WHAT YOU DO

- Prepare by threading the ring on the shoelace and tying the ends of the lace together in a simple knot.
- Tuck the ring and shoelace into your left vest pocket or the breast pocket of your jacket. The knotted ends should hang on the outside [FIG.1].

[FIG.1]

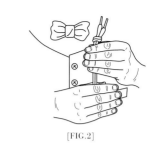

[FIG.2]

⚙ Take the knotted ends in your left hand and begin to pull the lace upward and out of your pocket. At the same time, your right hand (with its back toward the spectators) comes across and takes the center of the lace as it emerges. This is timed so that you conceal the ring from view [FIG.2].

⚙ Your right fingers should keep a light grip on the ring.

⚙ Still keeping hold of the ring and the center of the lace, bring your hands together in front of you and untie the knot. Pull the loop apart [FIG.3]. Display the lace and tug on it a couple of times.

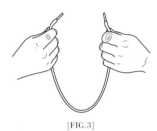

[FIG.3]

⚙ Tie the ends together again in a simple reef knot and display the loop [FIG.4].

⚙ The ring is still retained—hidden in the right fingers. You will find that you are able to execute the tying and untying operations quite easily without exposing the ring.

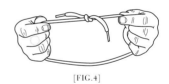

[FIG.4]

⚙ Make a tossing movement with both hands toward the center of the loop and at the same time release the palmed ring. It will seem to magically appear from thin air [FIG.5].

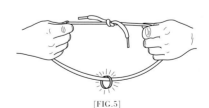

[FIG.5]

⚙ Untie the knot and display the ring on the shoelace by letting it run up and down the lace [FIG.6].

[FIG.6]

the ring and shoelace 2

Now that you've got your audience's attention, follow up with this trick, which makes their own jewelry deceive them.

WHAT THE TRICK IS

A ring is threaded onto a shoelace and yet, with both ends of the lace clearly visible, the ring is plucked from the center of the lace.

WHAT YOU NEED

A finger ring.
A long shoelace or string, about 33 inches/84 cm long.

WHAT YOU DO

○ Thread the ring onto the shoelace.
○ Take the ends in your left hand.
○ Insert the second and third fingers of your right hand (just these two—not the other two) through the loop, with the third finger resting on top of the ring [FIG.1].

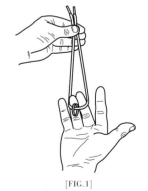

[FIG.1]

○ Bring your hand upward, palm toward the audience. Spread your fingers and display the ring in this position.

○ Lower your right hand again to the horizontal. Let your thumb come forward and grip the underside of the ring. The grip is now between this thumb and the third finger. Still holding the ends of the lace, bring the left hand down below the right; at the same time, turn the back of your right hand toward the audience [FIG.2].

○ Notice how the lace passes between your index and second fingers. These two fingers now take a grip on the lace and swing forward a little, creating a gap [FIG.3].

○ The left hand—back toward the audience—is inserted between the two hanging lengths of the lace and raised upward. The thumb goes through the gap that has just been created, while the fingers go behind the right index and second fingers [FIG.4].

○ The left hand continues to travel upward, taking the ends of the lace with it—thus secretly unthreading the ring [FIG.5]. As soon as the lace is clear of the ring, the right first and second fingers close the secret gap. The thumb and third finger still retain their hold on the ring.

○ Move your right hand away with a plucking action and show that you have magically removed the ring from the lace!

[FIG.2]

[FIG.3]

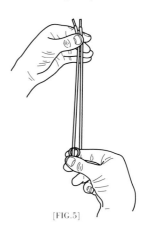

[FIG.4]

[FIG.5]

the cunning coin

There's nothing like the chink of coins to focus an audience's attention.

WHAT THE TRICK IS

You pluck a coin from a pile of coins, then open your hand to reveal that the coin has vanished.

WHAT YOU NEED

About a dozen coins.

WHAT YOU DO

- ✪ I want you to practice what you are supposed to do before I show you what you actually do. This is so that you get the timing and the psychology right.
- ✪ Have the coins in your right jacket or pant pocket.
- ✪ Take out all the coins and display them on your right palm [FIG.1].
- ✪ Reach over with your left hand and pick out one of the coins [FIG.2].

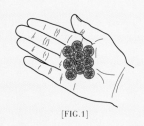

[FIG.1]

[FIG.2]

TIP

This trick may seem incredibly simple, but mastering the basic techniques is essential and they can be used as part of more complex magic.

- Close your left hand into a fist [FIG.3] and at the same time return the rest of the coins to your pocket.

- Open your left hand and show the coin [FIG.4].

- Okay? Right. Go through the motions two or three times. Now for the trick…

- Remove all the coins from your pocket.

- Reach over with your left hand as before, but this time just pretend to pick up a coin. Lift its edge, but let it drop again and come away swiftly, closing your left hand into a fist. Remember to keep the back of your hand facing the spectator.

- It will look for all the world as if you have taken a coin into your left hand.

- As you are now holding nothing in your left hand, it shouldn't be too difficult for you to make it disappear!

- Your acting skills come into play once again. Take your time—build up the suspense—then open your left hand to show that you have made the coin vanish.

[FIG.3]

[FIG.4]

> ★ Make sure that the match lands on a smooth, flat surface, or it could turn out to be an expensive trick!

the little match twirl

Who's going to refuse an offer like that? Then you throw the sucker punch...

WHAT THE TRICK IS

Matchbooks usually have advertising printed on one side only. You take a match and explain to the spectator that you will throw the match into the air. If it lands printed side up, you'll give them $10; if it lands blank side up, you'll only give them $2. You throw the match in the air... and it lands on its edge!

WHAT YOU NEED

A matchbook.

WHAT YOU DO

❂ Tear out a match and show that it has printing on one side only [FIG.1].

❂ *"Do you like a little gamble? Good! I am going to throw the match into the air. If it lands with the printed side*

ACE MATCHES

[FIG.1]

ACE MATCHES

[FIG.2]

up, I will give you $10. If it lands with the blank side up, I will give you $2."

❂ How can they lose? You'll pay them money regardless of which side the match falls. Are you mad?

❂ No, you're not mad. Before you throw the match up, bend it in half. It will always fall on its edge [FIG.2].

> ★ **Please take great care when performing this trick, because playing with fire is dangerous.**

the not-so-towering inferno

Always bet heavy on this one because you'll always be a winner.

WHAT THE TRICK IS

Setting three matches up as shown, you carefully set fire to the crossbar. You ask the spectator to bet on which of the two upright matches will ignite first. You'll buy them a drink if they guess correctly; if they're wrong, they must buy you a drink! They'll always be wrong!

WHAT YOU NEED

An empty matchbox and 3 matches.

WHAT YOU DO

- ○ Set three matches up as shown, by wedging one down each side with the heads upward, and the third wedged across the other two.
- ○ Carefully light the center of the crossbar match.

- ○ As the flame spreads, ask your spectator to bet which one of the two upright matches will catch fire first. They will be wrong—always!
- ○ Why? Long before the flame reaches the ends, the center match will jump into the air.

magic in the restaurant

RESTAURANTS PROVIDE an endless supply of items that can be used by the crafty magician. Knives, forks, spoons, napkins, glasses, sugar cubes, and wine bottles can all be utilized in our art. Your magic becomes completely impromptu—you just borrow all the props you need!

Your audience will be in a very good mood and susceptible to some superbly subtle magical entertainment. They are out to have a good time and a great meal. Your magic will be the icing on the cake!

The fact that you are seated is also a tremendous advantage. Sitting down enables you to learn the art of LAPPING—which is not a way of drinking. Lapping is when you use your lap to catch items that you secretly drop from your hand or the table edge. Your lap can also conceal items that you'll eventually produce with a magical flourish.

Don't try to involve restaurant diners on other tables in your magic. Magic is not compulsory, so please value their privacy. If they ask to join in—well, that's an entirely different matter. Be warned, though— if they have children on their table, they will disturb you for the rest of the evening.

These tricks are also great when you've been invited to dinner at the home of a friend or acquaintance. It can be annoying to be asked to "sing for your supper," but what can you do? As a magician, you'll just have to get used to it! Your reputation will precede you and your friends will always want you to perform your latest miracle. You'll get a buzz from their enjoyment of your entertainment, and plenty more dinner invites. So, devour the information on the following pages and look forward to many nights of magical meals.

the cut throat

You'll be cutting your own throat if your audience fails to swallow this piece of cunning cutlery conjuring.

WHAT THE TRICK IS

You pick up a table knife and swallow it. The knife is then made to reappear from your inside jacket pocket.

WHAT YOU NEED

A napkin.
A borrowed table knife.

WHAT YOU DO

* The napkin is on your lap.
* Lay the knife along the edge of the table and cover it with both your hands [FIG.1].

TIP

Allow your audience to see the knife the first time you appear to be raising it to your mouth. They will then assume that it is there the second time you raise your hands.

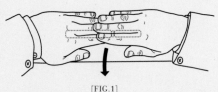

[FIG.1]

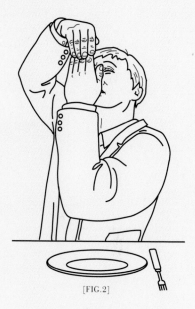

[FIG.2]

* Slide your hands back toward you, off the edge of the table, and then raise both hands to the position shown in FIG.2, holding the knife. Tilt your head back as if you are just about to swallow the knife.
* Cough and splutter a little as if the blade is choking you. Lay the knife along the edge of the table again.
* *"I think it needs a little salt!"*
* Pick up the salt cellar and sprinkle a little salt along the blade. Put the salt cellar back on the table.
* Put your hands over the knife again [FIG.1], making sure that there are no gaps between your fingers. Slide your hands off the edge of the table as before, but this time let the knife drop onto your lap on the top of the napkin.
* Pretend that you are holding the knife in your hands as you raise them back to the FIG.2 position.
* Pretend to slowly slide the knife down into your mouth by gradually lowering your hands and smacking your lips.
* Gesture with your hands, indirectly showing that they are empty.
* *"Wow! That tasted great!"*

* Pick up the napkin from your lap and wipe your mouth. Lay the napkin back in your lap and it will cover the knife from view.
* *"Waiter, could have another knife, please? I'm famished!"*
* Don't be in too much of a hurry to produce the knife. Let everyone sweat! When the heat is off, you can push the knife up and under the side of your jacket, transferring it to your inside pocket. You can then produce it when you're ready.

the looking glass

*Nobody will see through you if you
master this disappearing act.*

WHAT THE TRICK IS

A glass tumbler vanishes before your
audience's eyes.

WHAT YOU NEED

A coin.
A paper napkin.
A glass tumbler.

WHAT YOU DO

* Borrow a coin and place it on the table
  in front of you.
* Wrap the paper napkin around the
  tumbler so that it takes on the shape
  of the glass [FIG.1].
* *"I'm going to make this coin vanish.
  It has to be done in secret, so I will
  cover the coin with this glass and its
  cover. I will count to three and the
  coin will have completely disappeared:
  one—two—THREE!"*

[FIG.1]

* Lift up the glass and paper cover as one. The coin has not vanished [FIG.2].
* Replace the covered glass over the coin once again.
* *"Sorry! I'll have to try that once again. One—two—THREE!"*
* Lift the covered glass again and bring it back to the edge of the table. Lean forward, and gaze at the coin as if in total disbelief.
* *"I can't see where I'm going wrong…"*
* As you say this, let the tumbler secretly drop onto your lap. Keep hold of the napkin, gently, as if you are still holding the glass. The napkin will have retained the shape of the tumbler, so it will look very convincing.
* *"I'll try once more. Please watch very carefully. Blink and you'll miss it. One—two—THREE!"*
* Lift the napkin again. The coin is still there. Pause dramatically—then unravel the paper napkin.
* *"Oh! I'm sorry—this is the trick where the glass vanishes!"*
* Quickly reach down to your lap. Grab the tumbler and push it upward inside your jacket. Grip it with your upper arm and relax. After a suitable time interval you can reach into your jacket and appear to produce the glass from your inside pocket.

[FIG.2]

[FIG.3]

TIP

You are now in a position to perform the next trick (The Driller Killer Coin). The two tricks make an impressive routine.

the driller killer coin

Everyone is sure to lap up this delicious slice of dexterity.

WHAT THE TRICK IS

You press a borrowed coin onto the solid table. The coin magically passes through the table and is caught in a tumbler, which is held beneath. You then do it again, just to prove that it wasn't a fluke!

WHAT YOU NEED

A glass tumbler.
A borrowed coin.

WHAT YOU DO

* Sit at the table with your legs tucked well under it. The glass tumbler is on the table and to your left.
* Borrow a coin and place it on the table before you [FIG.1].

[FIG.1]

* *"I'm going to make this coin pass through the tablecloth, through the solid table, and into this glass!"*

* Place your right fingers over the coin [FIG.2] and pull it toward you. Let the coin drop onto your lap as your right hand continues backward and then upward as if it is holding the coin. Open your hand slightly as if you are looking at the coin [FIG.3].

* *"I'll place the glass under the table so that it catches the coin."*

* Pick up the glass with your left hand and take it beneath the table. Rest it on your knees and secretly locate the coin with your left hand.

* Slam your right hand onto the table.

* With your left hand, drop the coin sharply into the glass. The "clink" will be clearly heard. Lift up your right hand and show that the coin has gone. Get your timing right and it will appear that the coin has passed right through the table and landed with a clatter into the glass.

* Bring the glass out from under the table and pour the coin onto the table. Return it to its owner.

* You could pass a second coin through the table in a similar way. Execute a French Drop (*see page 24*). Drop your left hand to the edge of the table and let the coin drop onto your lap as you hold up your right fingers in pretense of holding the coin. Now carry on as before—passing the coin through the table and catching it in the glass.

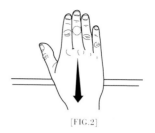

[FIG.2]

[FIG.3]

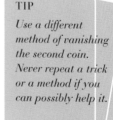

TIP

Use a different method of vanishing the second coin. Never repeat a trick or a method if you can possibly help it.

the matchmaker

Place this trick over a low flame, cook until charred, and serve with a glass of wine. It's a match made in heaven!

WHAT THE TRICK IS

A volunteer counts the number of matches in a matchbook. Let's say there are 19. One is torn out and struck. You blow out the flame and the match disappears. The spent match is found back in the matchbook—firmly affixed. There are still 19 matches in the book!

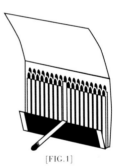

[FIG.1]

WHAT YOU NEED

A matchbook.

WHAT YOU DO

★ A little preparation is needed here. Pull back one of the matches [FIG.1], light it, and quickly blow out the flame. Tuck the book cover back in places but behind the dead match [FIG.2]. You are now ready to perform.

[FIG.2]

* Fold back the spent match and hide it under your left thumb [FIG.3]. Open the flap with your right fingers and ask your volunteer to count the number of matches [FIG.4].
* They say: "Nineteen."
* Tear out one of the center matches and then close the book in the following way. Revolve the whole book toward you and lay it, still open, flat on your left palm [FIG.5]. This action straightens out the hidden match, which now aligns with all the others.
* Pick up the book and—being careful not to expose the matches—tuck in the flap.
* Strike the match that you have torn out on the striking plate—then put the book on the table in full view.
* Shake out the flame after a couple of seconds—then make the match vanish using the French Drop (*see page 24*).
* Open your hand to show that the match has disappeared.
* *"Does anyone have a match? Mine seems to have vanished. Perhaps it went back in the book?"*
* DON'T TOUCH THE MATCHBOOK YOURSELF!
* Ask the volunteer to pick up the book and count the matches. There are still 19 matches, even though you tore one out after they were counted.
* Even more amazing is the fact that one of the matches appears to be the dead one that just vanished—and it's still affixed to the book!

[FIG.3]

[FIG.4]

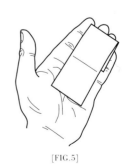

[FIG.5]

the olive switch

*This is a delicious aperitif apparition…
and you get to eat the props!*

WHAT THE TRICK IS

An olive is smacked onto the top of your head. It magically emerges from your mouth. You do it again, before devouring the evidence!

WHAT YOU NEED

A bowl of olives.

WHAT YOU DO

* Conceal an olive in your right hand. With the same hand, remove an olive from the bowl. Carry the olive to your mouth and hold it between your lips in full view [FIG.1].

* Pretend to take the olive from your lips with your right hand. In fact, let the olive you are displaying between your lips drop into your mouth and bring forward the olive that you have been concealing [FIG.2].

> **TIP**
>
> *Complete mastery of the French Drop and finger grips to conceal items is vital if you wish to perform these tricks perfectly. Revisit page 24 as necessary.*

[FIG.1]

* Now execute a French Drop (*see page 24*), while apparently moving the olive from your right to your left hand. Your right hand drops to the edge of the table and secretly drops the olive onto your lap.

* Slap your left hand down on top of your head.

* Maneuver the olive you are concealing in your mouth so that it appears between your lips again [FIG.1].

* Let the olive drop from your mouth down into your left hand.

* With your right hand, secretly pick up the olive that is on your lap. Conceal it in a finger grip.

* Use your right hand to pick up the olive from your left palm [FIG.3]. Bring your hand up to your mouth and apparently display this olive between your lips again. You actually push the visible olive into your mouth and move the finger-palmed olive up to be displayed between your lips.

* Let the visible olive drop from your mouth into your left hand. Appear to pick it up with your right hand, but execute a French Drop.

* Pretend to push the olive into your right ear [FIG.4]!

* Maneuver the olive that you are concealing in your mouth until you can display it between your lips again.

* Eat the evidence!

[FIG.2]

[FIG.3]

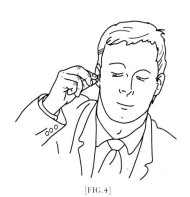

[FIG.4]

the cable car ring

Your dining partners will find this trick hard to digest. It's quite disturbing to watch gravity being bamboozled.

WHAT THE TRICK IS

A borrowed ring rides up a 30° slope in a most mysterious way—just like a cable car!

WHAT YOU NEED

A borrowed finger ring.
A thin rubber band. Snap it so that you are left with a straight strip of rubber.

TIP

Stop before the last bit of rubber emerges, or you will catapult the ring across the room! Tie a knot at one end so that you can feel when you've reached it.

WHAT YOU DO

* Thread the ring onto the rubber strip and lay it on the table.

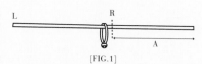

[FIG.1]

* Pick up the rubber strip at the points shown in FIG.1. The left finger and thumb grip at point "L." The right finger and thumb grip TIGHTLY at point "R" and stretch the rubber until the exposed piece is about the length of the original strip.

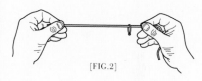

[FIG.2]

* The extra length that you have "stolen" ("A") is concealed in your right hand [FIG.2].

* Raise the left hand to create a slope of about 30°.

* Now, ease the pressure that your right thumb is exerting on the rubber band—VERY SLIGHTLY— allowing the concealed extra length to gradually pass through.

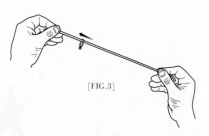

[FIG.3]

* The optical illusion is amazing. The ring will appear to travel up the slope in an extraordinary gravity-defying way [FIG.3].

the divine wine

Uncork this vintage trick and you'll be sure to make your companions whine.

WHAT THE TRICK IS

You show both sides of a napkin and then you produce a bottle of wine from its folds.

WHAT YOU NEED

A bottle of wine.
A cloth table napkin.

WHAT YOU DO

* Secretly hide the bottle under the left side of your jacket and tucked into the waistband of your pants.
* Grip the napkin by its top two corners and hold it out in front of you [FIG.1].
* Only use your thumbs and index fingers to grip, leaving your third and fourth fingers free. This is important.
* Show the other side of the napkin by crossing your hands. Notice that the right hand goes in front of the left hand [FIG.2].

[FIG.1]

[FIG.2]

[FIG.3]

* The next move shows *both* sides of the napkin again. Move your right hand in a clockwise direction to the right. Then continue moving the right hand round and back to the left so that the right hand is now behind the napkin [FIG.3].

* With your right hand concealed by the napkin, grip the top of the bottle with your third and fourth fingers.

* Breathe in. This will ease the pressure of your waistband on the bottle and allow you to lift it clear.

* As soon as you have a firm grip on the neck of the bottle, move your hand directly upward.

[FIG.4]

* The folds of the napkin will fall, draping around the bottle and concealing it from view [FIG.4].

* Move your right hand toward the center of the table, and place your left hand beneath the bottom of the concealed bottle

* Whisk the napkin away [FIG.5].

* *"Hey presto! Anyone for vino? Drinks are served!"*

[FIG.5]

the appearing disappearing coin

This recipe for serving up sleight of hand is easy to do and has a great effect on the audience! If the coin disappears, then your dinner guests won't!

WHAT THE TRICK IS

Showing your hands empty, you pluck a coin from your elbow. You rub the coin on your elbow and the coin suddenly disappears again.

WHAT YOU NEED

A large coin.

WHAT YOU DO

* Secretly tuck a large coin down the back of your shirt collar. It should stay there quite safely until you need it.
* Show both sides of your hands to your audience to emphasize that they are empty [FIG.1].

[FIG.1]

[FIG.2]

[FIG.3]

* Lean on your right arm. Bend your left arm and pluck at your left elbow with your right fingers as if looking for something [FIG.2]. This action brings your left fingers in line with the back of your collar. Steal the coin from your collar.

* Cover this furtive action by showing your right hand empty, having failed to find anything hidden in your left elbow [FIG.3].

[FIG.4]

* Now change sides and lean on your left elbow. Reach across and pluck at your right elbow with your left fingers [FIG.4]. "Produce" the coin magically from your elbow and display it for all to see [FIG.5].

* Now reverse the procedure and make the coin vanish! Perform a French Drop (*see page 24*), apparently taking the coin away in your right hand, but actually finger palming it in your left.

* Lean on your left elbow again [FIG.2]. Rub your right fingers (supposedly holding the coin) on your left elbow. Meanwhile, stick the coin down the back of your collar again!

* Display both sides of both hands to show that the coin has disappeared [FIG.1].

[FIG.5]

the lurking lemon

You need to be sharp to carry off this bitter-sweet surprise.

WHAT THE TRICK IS

You show your audience three coins. A spectator tries desperately to keep track of them, only to fail every time. Finally, the coins turn into a lemon!

WHAT YOU NEED

A small lemon (or a small onion or piece of fruit).
4 coins of the same value and appearance.

WHAT YOU DO

* Prepare by placing the lemon in your right jacket pocket and finger palming one of the coins in your right hand. The audience should never be aware of the fourth coin.

TIP

The technique of "two in my hand—one in my pocket" can be used with any small objects.

* Lay the remaining three coins out in a row on the table [FIG.1].
* *"I hope you all keep a close eye on your money. Watch me closely."*
* Pick up a coin with your right fingers and thumb. Toss it into your left hand.
* *"I'll put one in my hand…"*
* Pick up a second coin and toss it into your left hand. At the same time, release the palmed coin into your left hand too. Quickly close your left hand into a fist.
* *"…two in my hand…"*
* Pick up the third coin [FIG.2].
* *"…and the third one in my pocket."*
* Put your hand in your pocket, but instead of leaving the coin there, you finger palm it and bring your hand out again.
* *"How many coins are in my hand?"*
* *"Two."*
* *"No. Three!"*
* Lay the three coins out on the table. Now use your right hand once again to pick up a coin.

* *The Lurking Lemon trick is continued on the next page.*

[FIG.1]

[FIG.2]

the lurking lemon

* *"I'll do it again. I'll put one in my hand…"*
* Drop BOTH COINS into your left hand and quickly close it into a fist. Turn your fist over so that the thumb is at the top.
* Pick up the second coin and push it into the closed left fist between the thumb and first finger [FIG.3].
* *"…two in my hand…"*
* Pick up the last coin.
* *"…and the third one in my pocket."*
* Put it into your pocket. Leave it there and palm out the lemon.
* *"How many coins are in my hand?"*
* *"Two."*
* Lay out the three coins again.
* *"No. THREE! I will do it one more time."*

[FIG.3]

[FIG.4]

* Pick up the first coin with your right hand. Pretend to put the coin in your left hand, but hold on to it and drop the lemon into your hand instead.
* Quickly close your hand into a fist. If you do this casually but smartly, the lemon will not be seen. Honestly!
* The coin is not passed from hand to hand, but is drawn back into the right palm and hidden in a finger grip.
* Pick up the remaining two coins with the fingers of your right hand and drop all three into your pocket.
* *"How many coins am I holding in my left hand now?"*
* Whatever number they say, finish by slowly opening your left hand to show that the answer is a lemon [FIG.5].

[FIG.5]

the napkin kidnap

It's amazing what can happen beneath a napkin. With this trick, you'll have the money and the audience in your pocket.

WHAT THE TRICK IS
A borrowed coin is made to vanish from beneath a napkin.

WHAT YOU NEED
A borrowed coin—the larger the better.
A cloth table napkin.
A jacket with an outer breast pocket.

WHAT YOU DO
* Display the coin in the fingertips of your left hand at chest level [FIG.1].
* Drape the napkin up and over your left hand to conceal the coin [FIG.2]. With your right hand, pull the napkin across the concealed coin..
* Keep pulling the napkin over the coin

[FIG.1]

[FIG.2]

[FIG.3]

and your left hand. Your right hand, holding the napkin, comes to rest adjacent to your outer breast pocket as the coin, still held in your left fingers, comes into view again [FIG.3].

* Repeat the above actions, but as soon as your two hands come together, grip the coin between the thumb and index finger of your right hand.

* Steal the coin away hidden under cover of the napkin [FIG.4].

[FIG.4]

* The right hand continues toward your breast pocket as before. As soon as it reaches it, let the coin drop into your pocket [FIG.5].

* The napkin has now cleared your left hand, revealing that the coin has vanished. Show that both of your hands are empty and hand out the napkin for examination [FIG.6].

* Practice until the moves flow into one smooth, graceful sequence.

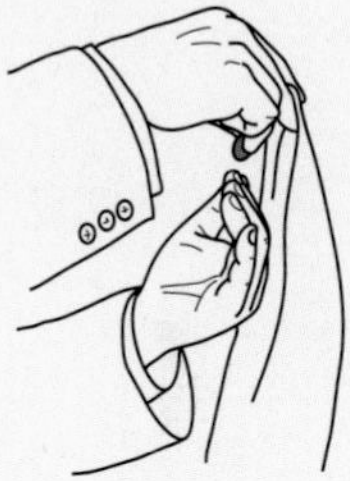

[FIG.5]

[FIG.6]

the sweet tooth

One sugar-cube or two? This trick is perfect for after-dinner coffee, and will leave your fellow guests shaken and stirred.

WHAT THE TRICK IS

You hold your left hand above your coffee cup and place a wrapped sugar-cube package on the back of your hand. You smack the package smartly with your right hand. The sugar cubes pass through your hand into your coffee cup, leaving the crushed wrapper behind. Sweet!

WHAT YOU NEED

A bowl of wrapped sugar cubes.

WHAT YOU DO

✱ Secretly steal a package of sugar cubes, then excuse yourself from the table. Retire to the washroom, and carefully unwrap the package [FIG.1]. Put the cubes in your pocket and reassemble the package. Moisten the final flap—it should stick down and the empty package will assume its former shape.

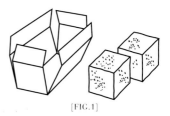

[FIG.1]

[FIG.2]

* Keep the empty sugar package hidden in your hand as you return to the dining table.
* Palm the sugar cubes in your left hand. Palm the empty wrapper in your right hand, being careful not to crush it. Just let it rest in your curled fingers.
* *"I've got an idea for a trick. Hand me a sugar-cube package."*
* Take the offered package between the thumb and index finger of your right hand. Place it on the table in front of you, about 2 inches/5 cm from the edge [FIG.2].
* Move your left fist over your coffee cup and at the same time sweep the visible sugar package toward you with your right hand.

[FIG.3]

* Let the package drop onto your lap and at the same time bring the empty sugar-cube wrapper into view and place it on the back of your left fist [FIG.3].
* Smack the back of your fist with your right hand, at the same time extending your left fingers—letting the sugar cubes drop into your coffee [FIG.4].
* It really looks as if the cubes have penetrated through your hand. Let your audience examine the crushed wrapper if they wish.
* If you have a sweet tooth, eat the cubes hidden on your lap.

[FIG.4]

the bread maker

Waiter! Not only is there a fly in my soup... there's a coin in my bread!

WHAT THE TRICK IS

You break open your bread roll and, amazingly, find a coin inside it!

WHAT YOU NEED

A coin—the larger the better.
A bread roll.

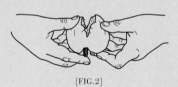

[FIG.1]

WHAT YOU DO

* Conceal the coin in your right hand. Pick up the bread roll with your left hand and place it in your right hand so that it covers the coin. You can now show both hands, apparently holding only the roll.
* Break open the roll from the top—opening it like a book [FIG.1].
* You will now be able to push the coin into the roll from underneath [FIG.2].
* *"HEY! What on earth is this?"*
* Fold out the roll [FIG.3]. Reach into the dough and remove the coin.
* Now watch the other diners frantically searching for money in their own rolls.

[FIG.2]

[FIG.3]

the ripper

They'll flock to see this wallpaper wonder. It will bring the house down!

WHAT THE TRICK IS

You point out to the restaurant owner that there is a terrible tear in the beautifully expensive wallpaper—then you magically repair it!

WHAT YOU NEED

White paper. Fold it in half and tear out a piece about 3 inches/8 cm long [FIG.1].

[FIG.1]

WHAT YOU DO

* Accordion-pleat one side of the paper [FIG.2]. Moisten the back of the other half and secretly press it firmly onto a stretch of wall where it will be noticed. Open up the pleated side a little and the illusion of ripped wallpaper is complete [FIG.3].

* After pointing it out to the restaurateur, go over to the wall and, with your back screening what you are doing, remove the paper. Screw it up into a ball and palm it.

* Now openly rub your hand over the area where the "rip" was and apparently heal it!

[FIG.2]

[FIG.3]

magic with cards

THERE ARE PROBABLY a hundred times more card tricks than all the other types of trick put together. This is because a deck of cards is so compact—slip a pack in your pocket and potentially you have an evening's entertainment at your fingertips. Playing cards also have a code of symbols and pictures—from a sinister black Ace to a lucky red Queen—that people recognize instantly, so putting them at their ease and hopefully off their guard.

Magicians are constantly "fiddling" with cards and coming up with new and fresh ideas and routines. Over the years, many magicians have earned a very good living with the aid of just those 52 magical cards! And those cards have over the centuries become synonymous with magic, with tricks such as "Find the Lady" a familiar feature of carnival chicanery.

Learn just two or three of the following tricks so that you can perform them "with your eyes closed." Intersperse them between other tricks so that your performance doesn't deteriorate into a series of "take-a-card" effects—you don't want to become predictable!

When you are buying playing cards for your tricks, it's useful to bear a few things in mind. I use poker cards, but the narrower bridge cards are also suitable—although they are not quite as visual. Choose packs with geometric patterns on the back, rather than pictures of dogs or cats. Remember that packs with white borders are best—some tricks require that a card be secretly reversed in the pack, and the white border acts as useful camouflage.

A final tip—always perform with a clean and healthy-looking pack. As soon as it gets even slightly worn, throw it away and buy a new one. You want the tools of your trade to be in perfect condition!

All the card tricks that follow will mystify your audience, although they are very easy to do. This will free you to devote your time and effort toward perfect prestidigitation and presentation.

the vocabulary of card tricks

Card magicians have a language all of their own and it's a good idea for you to familiarize yourself with some basic expressions.

FACE-UP CARD   FACE-DOWN CARD   FACE-UP DECK   FACE-DOWN DECK

TOP OF DECK   BOTTOM OF DECK

SHUFFLING

♣ To shuffle is to change the order of
all the cards in the pack. Hold the
cards in one hand, then lift up a
few from the bottom with the other
hand and throw them on top of the
rest. Keep doing this until you've
obtained a good mix.

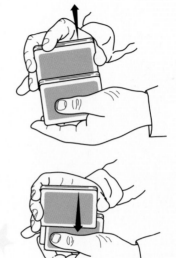

CUTTING

♣ Cutting is a simple way of changing
the order of the cards. Lift off some
of the cards (A) and place them to
one side.

♣ To complete the cut, pick up the
bottom half of the deck (B) and put
it on top of the rest (A).

the fairground fleece

This trick was originally used by con artists at fairgrounds and circuses. Your victim is likely to blow their big top!

WHAT THE TRICK IS

A spectator is so convinced that you have failed to find their chosen card that they are prepared to bet money on it. You then turn the tables in a spectacular way.

WHAT YOU NEED

A deck of cards.

WHAT YOU DO

♥ Give the deck to a volunteer to shuffle. Take it back, tilting the deck so that you can casually note the identity of the bottom card.

♥ Place the deck face down on the table.

♥ *"You've shuffled the deck, so no one— not even you—knows the order of the cards. Please look at the top card now and remember it. Then place it back on the top of the deck."*

TIP

Using a known card to help you locate an unknown card is called the KEY CARD principle. It is a widely used stratagem at the heart of many tricks!

💜 Cut the cards. This brings your volunteer's card near the center of the deck. More importantly, the original bottom card (the one you memorized) is now directly above their card.

💜 *"Would you like to cut the cards?"*

💜 They will usually accept your offer. If they don't, just give the deck another couple of complete cuts. This will not dislodge the two cards, merely change their location in the deck.

💜 *"I've learned to read the identity of the cards by touch. I'll show you."*

💜 Start to deal the cards slowly face up onto the table, one at a time [FIG.1]. Pretend to concentrate and "feel" each card before you turn it.

💜 Watch for the card that you originally remembered. The card after it will be the card that your volunteer chose. Feel the card—then deal it face up with the others as if it is of no interest to you. Deal three or four more cards face up, then stop—with the next card still held face down in your hand.

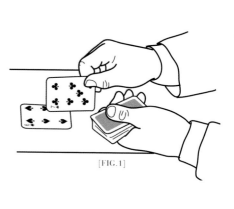

[FIG.1]

💜 *"That's it! I bet you $20 that the next card I turn over will be your card."*

💜 They'll think you're crazy because you've already dealt their card. This is the key to fleecing them.

💜 Once your volunteer accepts the bet, replace the card that you're holding on top of the deck. Take their card from those on the table [FIG.2].

💜 Turn the card face downward. You have done exactly as you promised!

💜 Take the money and run!

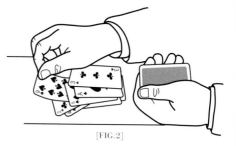

[FIG.2]

the mirror image

And now I'll read your mind. Oh dear, there's barely enough material there to make a short story!

WHAT THE TRICK IS

You and a spectator both choose cards from shuffled decks. It turns out that you've chosen the same card!

WHAT YOU NEED

2 decks of cards with backs of different colors.

WHAT YOU DO

♠ Place both decks on the table. Ask a volunteer to pick up either one. You pick up the other deck.

♠ *"This trick is called The Mirror Image. I want you to mirror my actions. Please shuffle the deck like this."*

♠ You both shuffle your decks [FIG.1].

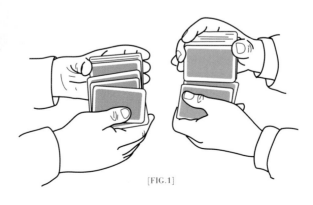

[FIG.1]

- As you finish shuffling, tilt the deck and secretly glimpse the bottom card. This will be easy as the volunteer will be engrossed with their own shuffling.

- *"We've both shuffled. I can't know the location of any card in your deck, and you can't know the location of any card in my deck. We'll swap decks."*

- You exchange decks.

- *"Reach into the center of the deck. Remove any card and remember it— then place it on the top of your deck. Don't let me see the card."*

- You do the same [FIG.2]. Don't bother to remember this card—only the original key card, which is on the bottom of your partner's deck.

- *"Cut the cards twice—like this. You are my mirror image. Remember to do exactly as I do."*

- Your volunteer follows you exactly.

- *"We'll exchange decks again. Look through this deck until you find your card. Remove the card and place it face down on the table. I'll do the same. Let me put my card down first so you know that I'm not cheating."*

- Exchange decks. Look through your deck until you locate the key card. The next card will be your volunteer's chosen card. Remove the card and place it face down on the table. Your mirror image places a card next to it.

- *"We shuffled both decks and we both chose a card at random. You are my mirror image, so the rules of mirror magic say we must have chosen the same card."*

- Let them turn over both cards [FIG.3]. They are identical: mirror images!

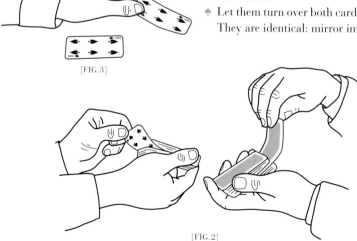

[FIG.3]

[FIG.2]

the untouchables

Look, no hands! It's the shuffle that holds the key to this mystifying magic.

WHAT THE TRICK IS

A volunteer cuts the deck to select a card. The deck is cut several times, then spread out, face down. You find the card without touching the deck.

WHAT YOU NEED

A deck of cards.
A pencil.

WHAT YOU DO

◆ Secretly prepare for this trick by making a "key card": mark any card on the back with a pencil dot in the white border, top left and bottom right [FIG.1]. Place this key card as the 26th card in the deck.
◆ Place the deck on the table.
◆ *"Cut the pack into three, like this."*
◆ Demonstrate by lifting two-thirds of the deck and placing it to the right. Lift half the cards from this pile and place these to the right again.

TIP

If you reach the right-hand end of the spread before you have counted 26, continue your count from the left-hand end. The card will always be 26 cards away.

[FIG.1]

◆ Reassemble the deck as it was before and ask your volunteer to cut the pack in the same way. We'll call the original bottom pile A, the middle pile B, and the original top pile C [FIG.2].

◆ Your key card will be in pile B.

◆ Point to pile C.

◆ *"Shuffle this pile so that nobody knows the order of the cards."*

◆ They shuffle. Then ask them to look at the top card, remember it, and replace it on top of the pile.

◆ Point to pile B.

◆ *"Place your cards on top of this pile."*

◆ Point to pile A.

◆ *"Shuffle this pile—then place them on top of the other cards."*

◆ Your volunteer's card will now be 26 cards away from your key card!

◆ *"Cut the deck twice."*

◆ Ensure they are cuts, not shuffles.

◆ *"I haven't touched the cards. You've shuffled twice and cut the deck. It's impossible for me to know your card."*

◆ Ask them to spread the deck face down across the table. Make sure that the edge of every card shows [FIG.3].

◆ *"Hold my left wrist. I am going to try to receive 'impulses' from you."*

◆ Starting from the LEFT side, move the index finger of your right hand along the line of cards, about 2 inches/5 cm above them. When you spot your key card, silently count this as No.1, and continue to count the cards silently until you reach 26.

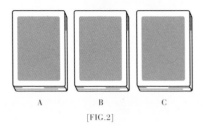

A   B   C

[FIG.2]

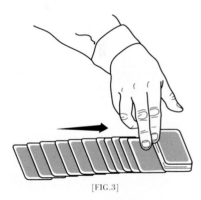

[FIG.3]

◆ This card will be their chosen card.

◆ When your index finger is over this card, wiggle your left hand as if you are receiving impulses from your volunteer!

◆ Ask the volunteer to pull the card out of the spread, and leave it face down on the table.

◆ *"What card did you choose?"*

◆ Let them turn the card over...

the lady vanishes

This is a smart version of the old racecourse con, Find The Lady. It will always get you past the winning post.

WHAT THE TRICK IS

A Queen and two other cards are shown. The spectator is asked to keep a sharp eye on the Queen. No matter how hard they concentrate, they always fail to find the Queen.

WHAT YOU NEED

2 matching decks of cards.

WHAT YOU DO

♣ To prepare, take the Q♠ from the first deck, and cut it into three equal sections. Discard the central section and tape the top and bottom sections together [FIG.1].

♣ Note that one part of the card is face up—the other face down. Leave a small gap between the sections, about the thickness of a playing card.

♣ Slide the hinged Queen over the end of a Joker from the first deck [FIG.2].

[FIG.1]

[FIG.2]

- Place this trick Joker between two Aces from the first deck.
- Put the Q♠ from the second deck into your inside left jacket pocket.
- Display the cards in your left hand as shown [FIG.3], with the hinged Queen obscuring the top of the Joker.
- "*I have three cards—two Aces and a Queen. Keep your eye on the Queen.*"
- Pass the cards into your right hand and hold them squared up [FIG.4], with the hinge now nearest your wrist.
- With the fingers of your left hand, pull out the bottom card (an Ace) and place it face down on the table.
- Pull out the new bottom card (the Joker) and place it face down next to the first card. The Joker will pull clear of the hinged Queen, which must remain hidden in your right hand.
- Place the last card face down.
- Slowly move the cards around.
- "*Keep a sharp eye on the Queen.*"
- Ask your victim to turn over the card that they think is the Queen.
- It's the Joker!
- Turn over the other two cards to show that they are Aces. The lady vanishes!
- Reach into your left jacket pocket, dump the hinged card, and produce the Queen.

TIP

I keep my set of trick cards in an envelope in my wallet so that I'm always ready to perform this fancy fairground trick.

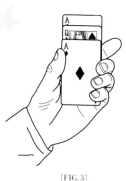

[FIG.3]

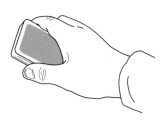

[FIG.4]

the red-hot poker

Keep wearing that poker face, as you deal yourself a winning hand every time.

WHAT THE TRICK IS

You offer to deal a few hands of poker. The spectator loses every time—even when they deal the cards themselves!

WHAT YOU NEED

Ten cards: 10♥, 9♥, 9♦, 9♠, 7♥, 7♣, 7♠, 6♥, 6♦, 6♠.

WHAT YOU DO

♥ Prepare in a similar way to The Untouchables (*see page 102*). Place a small pencil dot in the top-left and bottom-right corners of the margin on the back of the 10♥.

♥ FACT: Any poker hand dealt from these cards will lose if it contains the 10♥.

♥ Show your opponent what cards you are playing with. Shuffle until you see the pencil dots, indicating that the 10♥ is the top face-down card.

♥ *"We're going to play poker with a reduced deck of cards. Whatever happens, I will never lose!"*

ORDER OF WINNING HANDS

Full house
(beats three of a kind)

Three of a kind
(beats two pairs)

Two pairs
(beats one pair)

💜 Deal two poker hands of five cards each. Your opponent gets the first card, you get the second, they get the third, and so on.

💜 Both lay down your hands face up on the table. You will see that you have the strongest poker hand.

💜 The 10💜 should be the top card of your rival's five face-up cards [FIG.1].

💜 Drop your five cards on top of these, turn the cards face down, and deal them out.

💜 You win again. The 10💜 should now be the middle card of your opponent's hand [FIG.2].

💜 Drop your five cards on top of your rival's cards. Turn them face down and deal again.

💜 You win!

💜 Give your opponent all ten cards.

💜 *"Shuffle them thoroughly, and deal out the two hands. Just remember that I never lose!"*

💜 Watch for the pencil dots. These will tell you which hand contains the 10💜. You don't want this hand.

💜 If you see that your opponent has the 10💜 hand, just carry on as before. Turn your cards up to show that you have won yet again—even though you didn't shuffle or deal!

💜 However, if your opponent has dealt the dotted card to you, speak quickly before looking at the cards.

💜 *"I'm going to be even fairer this time. Point to one of the hands."*

[FIG.1]

[FIG.2]

💜 If your opponent points to the one that contains the dotted card, let them pick up the cards. You pick up the other hand and proceed as before.

💜 If your opponent points to the other hand, YOU PICK IT UP.

💜 *"You shuffled, and dealt, and even chose the hand I should play with…"*

💜 Lay down your cards.

💜 *"…but I win again!"*

the king's prophecy

If you could see into the future, everyone would treat you like a king. But prepare carefully or you'll look like a joker!

WHAT THE TRICK IS

You bet your victim $20 that you can see into the future and predict which card they will select, even before they choose it. Not only do you reveal the correct card, but its name is written on your $20 bill!

WHAT YOU NEED

A $20 bill.
A wallet.
A deck of cards.

WHAT YOU DO

♠ Secretly prepare for this trick by writing on the back of a $20 bill in big letters: "KING OF HEARTS."

♠ Put the $20 bill in your wallet. Take the K♥ from your deck and slide it behind the $20 note.

TIP

The secret of this great trick's success is that you appear to predict your victim's choice, when in fact you are actually forcing that choice by using a hidden card.

♠ Put the wallet in your pocket. You are ready to introduce the trick.

♠ *"As a magician, I find it very useful that I can see into the future. I can often tell what people will do before they do it."*

♠ Give your victim the deck of cards and insist that they shuffle it thoroughly before placing the deck face down on the table.

♠ Take out your wallet and remove the $20 bill with the K♥ concealed beneath it. The writing should be hidden on the back of the note. Be careful not to expose the card.

♠ *"Cut the deck. I bet you $20 that I know what card you will cut to!"*

♠ They may or may not accept the bet. Either way, ask them to cut the deck.

♠ Place the $20 bill on top of the lower half of the deck, adding the concealed K♥ to the top of the pile [FIG.1]. Pick up the other half of the deck and place it on top of the $20 bill [FIG.2].

♠ *"I said I knew what you'd do before you did it. Well—you shuffled the deck thoroughly and cut the cards exactly where you wanted to. Now lift up the cards*

[FIG.1]

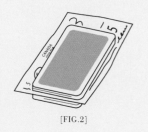

[FIG.2]

that are on top of the note and put them to one side."

♠ They do this.

♠ *"Pick up the $20 note. Turn it over and read what's written on it."*

♠ They read: "KING OF HEARTS."

♠ Point to the top card of what was the lower half of the deck.

♠ *"Turn over the card that you originally cut to."*

♠ It is, of course, the King of Hearts!

the shepherd and his flock

This easy but impressive card trick will have people flocking back for more!

WHAT THE TRICK IS

A spectator helps you assemble the pack of cards so that half is face down and the other is half face up. With a snap of the fingers you make all the face-up cards turn over so that the complete pack is the right way round once again.

[FIG.1]

WHAT YOU NEED

A deck of cards.

WHAT YOU DO

♦ Prepare for this trick by secretly turning over the bottom card so that it is face up [FIG.1].

TIP

If you begin by secretly reversing TWO cards you can instantly repeat the trick. The sheer simplicity will fool people a second time.

- Spread the face-down pack between your hands to show casually that the cards are all facing the same way. Be careful not to expose your reversed bottom card!
- Square the pack up and place it on your left palm.
- Invite a volunteer to lift off about half of the cards [FIG.2].
- You now have to do two things at once! Stay calm!
- 1. Ask the person who cut the cards to turn their cards face up.
- 2. At the same time, CASUALLY turn your left hand over so that what was the bottom card of your pile is now the top card. It still looks as if your half of the deck is face down [FIG.3]. Your volunteer will be so busy concentrating on their own cards that they won't notice what you've done.
- Take the face-up pile from your volunteer and place the cards beneath your (apparently) face-down half.
- Turn the completed deck over THREE TIMES as you talk to them.
- *"We now have half of the pack face down and the other half face up."*
- The THREE TURNS will bring the one reversed card back to its original position on the bottom of the deck. Now place the deck on your left palm once again.
- *"Did you know that cards are just like sheep? I'll take one of the face-up cards and turn it face down."*

[FIG.2]

[FIG.3]

- With your right fingers, take the bottom card and place it face down on top of the deck.
- *"When one card moves the rest follow—listen to them go!"*
- Hold the pack up to the volunteer's ear and run your thumb along the edge of the cards to cause a "rippling" sound. Now spread the cards across the table to show that they are all the same way round again.
- *"What did I tell you? Just like sheep!"*

the fingertip flip

This is one trick that you really will have to learn to do with your eyes closed.

WHAT THE TRICK IS

The spectator's chosen card is found to be the only reversed card in the whole deck.

WHAT YOU NEED

A deck of cards.

> ### TIP
>
> *Perfect your patter to divert the spectator's attention away from the cards while you manipulate the deck.*

WHAT YOU DO

♣ Begin by secretly reversing the bottom card of the deck (as in the previous trick). Put the deck back in the box and you are ready to perform.

♣ Tip out the cards and spread them between your hands to have the spectator remove one. Be careful not to expose the reversed bottom card.

♣ Once they remove the card, square the deck and turn your wrist over to bring the bottom of the deck to the top as they study the card. It will still look as if the deck is face down because of the reversed card.

♣ Grip the deck firmly and have them put the card back into the center of the deck [FIG.1]. Release the pressure just enough to allow them to insert the card, but avoid the cards spreading and revealing that the pack is really face up.

♣ Place the pack behind your back.

♣ "I'm going to attempt to find your card with only the aid of my trained and very sensitive fingertips!"

♣ Turn your original face-down card over so that it is face up. Now there is only one reversed card in the deck. It is near the center and is the victim's chosen one!

[FIG.1]

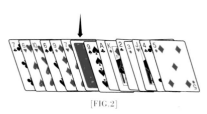

[FIG.2]

♣ Bring the deck into view again and widely spread the cards FACE UP across the table. One card will show up face down in the center of the face-up deck [FIG.2]. Point to it and say:

♣ *"I've just turned over one card in the center of the deck. What was the name of your card?"*

♣ "The Four of Spades."

♣ *"Please turn the card over."*

♣ The spectator's face will be a picture and you have found the card without ever knowing which one it was!

the one-way deck

It's the picture that tells the story in this very neat trick.

WHAT THE TRICK IS

I always advise budding magicians to use cards with geometric and thus reversible back designs [FIG.1]. However, a deck with a picture on it [FIG.2] makes several neat tricks possible. Here, a spectator chooses a card, returns it to the deck, and then thoroughly shuffles the cards. You are still able to find their card!

WHAT YOU NEED

A one-way deck.

[FIG.1]

[FIG.2]

WHAT YOU DO

- ♥ Make sure that all the cards are facing the same way before you begin.
- ♥ Fan or spread the cards out so that the spectator can choose one. Emphasize that they have a completely free choice.
- ♥ As they are looking at their card, secretly turn the pack 180°—then spread the cards out again for the return of the card. As long as the spectator hasn't turned his card around too, it will now be the only one with a disoriented back. To you it will appear obvious!

- ♥ Once the card has been safely returned, ask them to shuffle the deck thoroughly so that the card is completely lost and nobody (not even the spectactor) knows where it is.
- ♥ Take the deck back and, holding the cards up with the faces toward the spectator, thumb through the cards. Ask the spectator to focus hard when they see their card, but to try not to give you any signals.
- ♥ The backs are toward you and they can't see them. You will soon spot the card [FIG.3]. Don't pull it out straight away. Make it look difficult—go past it and then start again, finally lifting the card right out of the deck and displaying it with a flourish!

[FIG.3]

the lazy magician

Take it easy with this trick and let the spectactor do all the hard work.

WHAT THE TRICK IS

The spectator cuts the deck into four piles and then does a little card mixing. When finished, they turn over the top card of each pile and to their amazement discover that they have found the four Aces!

WHAT YOU NEED

A deck of cards.

WHAT YOU DO

♠ Place the four Aces on top of the deck before you start [FIG.1].

♠ Ask the spectator to cut the deck into four fairly equal piles. Keep your eye on where the top quarter with the Aces ends up.

♠ Arrange the four piles in a row, ensuring that the "Aces" pile is the fourth pile [FIG.2].

TIP

Although the starring role in this trick belongs to the spectator, you must ensure that they follow your directions accurately.

♠ *"This is pile one, pile two, pile three, and pile four."*

♠ From now on do not touch the cards. The spectactor does the work!

♠ Point to pile one.

♠ *"Pick up this pile, please. I want you to transfer three cards from the top of the pile to the bottom of the pile. Then you must deal one card onto each of the other three piles."*

♠ When that's done, have them put the pile back where it was and pick up pile two. Ask them to transfer three cards from the top to the bottom and then to deal a card onto each of the other three piles. They then return the pile to position two.

♠ The spectator repeats the action with the other piles. There should now be an Ace on top of each pile. Say:

♠ *"You look like a poker player to me! You shuffled and cut the cards yourself. I didn't touch the cards once, so let's see how good you are. Turn over the top card of each pile. Wow! That's a spectacular climax!"*[FIG.3]

[FIG.1]

[FIG.2]

[FIG.3]

the last two cards match

There's a stunning climax to this trick that will have your audience doubled up.

WHAT THE TRICK IS

Five playing cards are torn in half to make ten half cards [FIG.1]. The spectator assists you in a spelling game using the half cards to represent letters. Although they have complete control of every move, the half cards always manage to find their other halves!

WHAT YOU NEED

Five old playing cards. I've used Ace to 5 to make the explanation easier to follow, but the effect is better if you use five random cards. Tear them neatly across their centers.

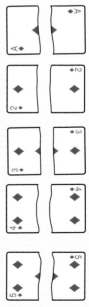

[FIG.1]

WHAT YOU DO

♦ From the starting point [FIG.1], gather up the left-hand pieces—then the right. Put one pile on top of the other. It is important that the running order of the five halves is the same, so from the top you should now have A, 2, 3, 4, 5, A, 2, 3, 4, 5.

[FIG.2]

♦ With the pile of half cards held face down, deal off five cards from the top onto a pile on the table. This reverses their order. Place the remaining five half cards to the left of this pile [FIG.2].

♦ *"This trick is called 'Last two cards match'—what is it called?"*

♦ "Last two cards match."

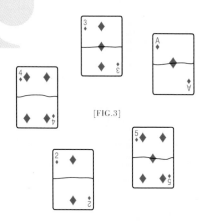

[FIG.3]

♦ *"We're going to spell out the name of the trick 'LAST TWO CARDS MATCH' using a piece of half card to represent each letter, and YOU have to tell me which half cards to use. Which pile shall I pick up?"*

♦ They point to a pile. Pick it up.

♦ *"The first word is 'LAST'. That's 'L'..."*

♦ Transfer one card from the top to the bottom of the five that you are holding.

♦ *"The next letter is 'A.' Shall I continue with this pile or use the other pile?"*

♦ Do exactly as they ask. If they want you to use the other pile, put down the pile that you're holding and transfer one card from the top to the bottom of the other pile. Give them the choice of piles for "S" and "T."

♦ After the letter "T" has been spelled, take one card from the top of each pile and place them together aside.

♦ Continue to spell out the words TWO CARDS MATCH in the same way— remembering to place a pair of cards aside as each word is completed.

♦ You will be left with two half cards.

♦ *"What is the name of the trick?"*

♦ "Last two cards match."

♦ Turn your two halves face up. They are a perfect match!

♦ The spectator thinks the trick is over, but you have an extra surprise for them!

♦ Turn over the other four pairs of cards. They all match too [FIG.3]!

the chased but never caught

A classic, this trick requires sleight of hand and an Oscar-winning performance.

WHAT THE TRICK IS

A spectator removes any Club, Heart, Spade, and Diamond from the pack. You ask them merely to keep one card in mind. You put the cards in your jacket pocket. After considerable concentration, you remove three of the cards, then ask the spectactor to name the card they were thinking of. You remove the final card from your pocket. It's the spectactor's card!

WHAT YOU NEED

A deck of cards.

TIP

The spectator will not realize that you still have three cards in your pocket at the end of the trick. You are now in a position to repeat the trick if you wish!

WHAT YOU DO

- ♣ Secretly place any three cards in your jacket pocket before you start. Lay them on their long sides at the bottom of the pocket.

- ♣ You must remember the key word CHASED. This is a mnemonic representing C (Clubs), H (Hearts), A, S (Spades), E, D (Diamonds).

- ♣ Spread the deck of cards out face upward and ask the spectator to remove any Club, any Heart, any Spade, and any Diamond. Put the rest of the deck aside.

- ♣ Arrange them in the CHASED order and then fan them out for the spectator to see [FIG.1].

[FIG.1]

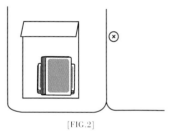

[FIG.2]

- ♣ "*You've chosen four cards at random. I want you to think of just ONE of them. Don't say which one—just think of it. OK?*"

- ♣ Place the four cards in your jacket pocket, this time standing them on their short ends so that you can tell them apart from the secret three that are already in your pocket [FIG.2].

- ♣ Now go for that Oscar-winning performance!

- ♣ "*Please concentrate a little harder. This isn't a game of chance. I'm really attempting to read your thoughts.*"

- ♣ Reach into your pocket and remove one of the secret three cards. Do not show its face.

- ♣ "*I don't think it's this one.*"

- ♣ Remove another one.

- ♣ "*You're not thinking of this one either...*"

- ♣ Remove the third secret card. Take care not to show the faces of the secret cards.

- ♣ "*...nor this one.*"

- ♣ Put your hand back into your pocket.

- ♣ "*That just leaves me with one card. What's the name of the card that you're thinking of?*"

- ♣ They name their card. Take out the correct one with a flourish!

the color match

This slick trick will dupe even the most eagle-eyed of spectactors.

WHAT THE TRICK IS

You shuffle the deck, then spread the cards face down across the table. The spectator is invited to pull any card toward them. You do the same. You turn the two cards face up—they're the same color. You repeat this about ten times. If they choose black—you've chosen black too. If their card is red—so is yours.

WHAT YOU NEED

A deck of cards.

TIP

Be confident in your own powers of observation: the smallest suggestion of a bend will be enough for you to identify the reds from the blacks.

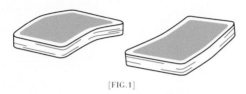

[FIG. 1]

WHAT YOU DO

💜 Prepare by separating the red and black cards.

💜 Give the red cards a very slight concave bend.

💜 Give the black cards a very slight convex bend [FIG. 1].

💜 Now loosely shuffle the red and black cards together without destroying their secret bends. Spread the cards out across the table so that most, if not all, of them are separated.

💜 Ask the spectator to put their finger on any card. You should be able to tell which way it bends. Look for a card with a similar bend on the other side of the table. Put your finger on it and drag it toward you.

💜 Ask the spectator to turn their card face up. You turn yours over too. They are the same color, say red.

💜 Have the spectator pick out another card. Again, match the bend and you will automatically match their color.

💜 Don't fall into the trap of going through the whole deck. Ten or twelve pairs will be quite enough.

💜 At the end of your demonstration, gather all the cards in and give them a thorough shuffling—thus flattening out the bends and destroying the incriminating evidence!

the name game

A card magic classic that blows a smoke screen of deception.

WHAT THE TRICK IS

A spectator places a random card in each jacket pocket. You successfully name the two cards!

WHAT YOU NEED

A deck of cards.

WHAT YOU DO

★ You must secretly memorize the third and fourth cards from the bottom of the deck. You could make it easier for yourself by putting the 3♣ and the 4♠ in these positions [FIG.1]. You now only have to remember the suits. Have a look at THE CHASED BUT NEVER CAUGHT (*page 121*).

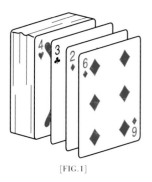

[FIG.1]

♠ Get the spectator to cut the pack into two fairly equal halves and POINT to one. Don't say "CHOOSE." You want them to end up with the original bottom half of the pack. If they point to it, have them pick it up. If they point to the other pile, YOU PICK IT UP and offer them the other one!

♠ *"I want you to duplicate every action that I do. Will you count your cards, and I'll count mine."*

♠ You count your cards by dealing them face down one at a time onto a pile on the table. The spectator does the same. Your two noted cards will now be the third and fourth cards from the top of their pile.

♠ Tell them how many cards you have and have them announce how many they have. Pretend that the number has some relevance to the trick. Ask them to discard one card. They will naturally throw away their top card.

♠ *"Please continue to follow my actions."*

♠ Take the top card of your pile and slide it into the center of your cards.

♠ Take a card off the bottom and slide it into the center too. Wait while they do the same.

♠ Take a card from the top and place it in your left jacket pocket.

♠ Take another card from the bottom and push it into the center.

♠ Take another card from the top and place it in your right jacket pocket.

♠ Place the rest of your cards on the table.

♠ These actions have been deliberately designed to create a smoke screen of misdirection. If the spectator has been following you, they should now have the 3♣ in their left pocket and the 4♠ in their right!

♠ You end the trick like this:

♠ *"It is a gambling certainty that this card in my right jacket pocket being the …"* [Name it as you show it.] *"… the card in your LEFT jacket pocket will be the THREE OF CLUBS!"*

♠ They take it out and show it.

♠ *"And this one in my other pocket being the …"* [Remove the card and name it as you show it.] *"… the one in your other pocket will definitely be the FOUR OF HEARTS! Am I right?"*

magic in the future

"...and for my next trick?"

MAGICIANS GUARD their secrets jealously. So why am I giving away so many of them in this book? The answer is very simple: the art of presenting magic takes hard work and dedication, and new magicians learn best from experienced performers. This book is intended to stimulate, educate, and entertain as well as to encourage magic hobbyists to pursue a fun, fulfilling pastime.

The tricks in *Magic Tricks for Grown-Ups* represent the first step along the road—they involve little or no sleight of hand. Your next step will be to learn a degree of digital dexterity. The following books can help you to achieve this. They can all be ordered from your local bookseller, or online through www.amazon.com

THE ROYAL ROAD TO CARD MAGIC by Jean Hugard & Frederick Braue. Dover Publications, 1999.

MODERN MAGIC MANUAL by Jean Hugard. First published in 1939 with regular reprints. Search online or in a used bookstore.

MARK WILSON'S COMPLETE COURSE IN MAGIC by Mark Wilson. Running Press, 2003.

… and, of course, any of my other magic books!

An online search for "Magic" will yield a wealth of websites that recommend or sell books, videos, DVDS, and props online, such as www.MagicWorldOnline.com

Also visit www.jontremaine.co.uk for an online demonstration of some close-up magic!

MAGIC: THE MAGAZINE FOR MAGICIANS This superb monthly magazine includes interviews with the world's foremost magicians, topical news, reviews and features, events listings and the latest new tricks.

You can find it online at www.magicmagazine.com

FINALLY

Find out if there is a Magic Club in your area and join it! You will learn much in the company of other magicians.

JON TREMAINE

index